First World War
and Army of Occupation
War Diary
France, Belgium and Germany

40 DIVISION
Divisional Troops
Royal Army Veterinary Corps
51 Mobile Veterinary Section
4 June 1916 - 31 March 1919

WO95/2603/2

The Naval & Military Press Ltd
www.nmarchive.com
Published in association with The National Archives

Published by

The Naval & Military Press Ltd

Unit 10 Ridgewood Industrial Park,

Uckfield, East Sussex,

TN22 5QE England

Tel: +44 (0) 1825 749494

www.naval-military-press.com

www.nmarchive.com

This diary has been reprinted in facsimile from the original. Any imperfections are inevitably reproduced and the quality may fall short of modern type and cartographic standards.

© Crown Copyright
Images reproduced by permission of The National Archives, London, England, 2015.

Contents

Document type	Place/Title	Date From	Date To
Heading	WO95/2603/2 51 Mobile Veternary Section		
Heading	40th Division 51st Mobile Vety Section Jun 1916-Mar 1919		
War Diary	Deepcut	04/06/1916	04/06/1916
War Diary	Southampton.	04/06/1916	04/06/1916
War Diary	Havre.	05/06/1916	06/06/1916
War Diary	Lillers.	07/06/1916	07/06/1916
War Diary	Amettes	07/06/1916	10/06/1916
War Diary	Lagoulee.	11/06/1916	18/06/1916
War Diary	Lagoullee Bruay.	19/06/1916	19/06/1916
War Diary	Bruay	20/06/1916	30/06/1916
Heading	War Diary of Capt G.C. Lancaster AVC. O.C 51 M.V.S. 40 Div From July 1-July 31. 1916		
War Diary	Bruay	01/07/1916	03/07/1916
War Diary	Drouvin	04/07/1916	31/08/1916
War Diary	Drouvin Reference Map 36B K.4.c.	01/09/1916	11/09/1916
War Diary	Drouvin	12/09/1916	24/09/1916
War Diary	Gonnehem.	24/09/1916	24/09/1916
War Diary	Drouvin.	24/09/1916	31/10/1916
War Diary	Roellecourt	01/11/1916	04/11/1916
War Diary	Frohen-Le-petit	05/11/1916	06/11/1916
War Diary	Bernaville	07/11/1916	15/11/1916
War Diary	Frohen-Le-Petit.	16/11/1916	19/11/1916
War Diary	Bouque-Maison	20/11/1916	22/11/1916
War Diary	Doullens	23/11/1916	23/11/1916
War Diary	Canaples	24/11/1916	24/11/1916
War Diary	Ailly-Le-Haut. Clocher	25/11/1916	25/11/1916
War Diary	Famechon	26/11/1916	13/12/1916
War Diary	St. Sauveur	13/12/1916	13/12/1916
War Diary	Vaux-Sur-Somme.	15/12/1916	15/12/1916
War Diary	Chipilly	16/12/1916	26/12/1916
War Diary	Bray-Sur-Somme	27/12/1916	30/01/1917
War Diary	Chipilly	01/02/1917	11/02/1917
War Diary	Bray	12/02/1917	09/03/1917
War Diary	Suzanne	10/03/1917	23/03/1917
War Diary	Curlu	24/03/1917	31/03/1917
War Diary	Moislains	23/04/1917	23/04/1917
War Diary	Curlu	07/04/1917	07/04/1917
War Diary	Moislains	08/04/1917	14/04/1917
War Diary	Curlu.	02/04/1917	06/04/1917
Diagram etc	Sheet 62c. Appendix I		
Miscellaneous	Extract From Report By Captain G.C. Lancaster, A.V.C. on The Treatment of Ulcerative Cellulitis By The Injection of Turpentine Appendix II		
Miscellaneous	Routine Orders by Major General H.G. Ruggles-Brise, C.B., M.V.O., Commanding 40th Division Appendix III		
War Diary	Moislains Map Reference Sheet 62 CC12c7,5.	01/05/1917	09/05/1917
War Diary	Moislains	10/05/1917	30/05/1917
Miscellaneous	Appendix I		

War Diary	Moislains (Sheet. 62c-C12)	01/06/1917	04/06/1917
War Diary	Moislains	05/06/1917	11/10/1917
War Diary	Bapaume	12/10/1917	12/10/1917
War Diary	Monchiet	13/10/1917	29/10/1917
War Diary	Warlincourt Les-pas	30/10/1917	18/11/1917
War Diary	Achiet-Le-Petit.	18/11/1917	20/11/1917
War Diary	Le. Transloy	20/11/1917	24/11/1917
War Diary	Ruyalcourt	25/11/1917	27/11/1917
War Diary	Bapaume	28/11/1917	28/11/1917
War Diary	Basseuy	29/11/1917	03/12/1917
War Diary	Boiry-St-Rictrude	04/12/1917	31/12/1917
War Diary	Boiry-St. Martin	01/01/1918	28/02/1918
War Diary	Bellacourt	01/03/1918	03/03/1918
War Diary	Monchiet	04/03/1918	13/03/1918
War Diary	Hendecourt	14/03/1918	22/03/1918
War Diary	Adinfer	23/03/1918	27/03/1918
War Diary	St. Amand	28/03/1918	28/03/1918
War Diary	Humbercourt	29/03/1918	29/03/1918
War Diary	Herlin-Le-Vert.	30/03/1918	31/03/1918
War Diary	Lillers	01/04/1918	01/04/1918
War Diary	Trou-Bayard	02/04/1918	08/04/1918
War Diary	Rue-De-Bois.	09/04/1918	11/04/1918
War Diary	Borre	12/04/1918	12/04/1918
War Diary	Hondeghem.	13/04/1918	14/04/1918
War Diary	Longuenesse.	15/04/1918	21/04/1918
War Diary	Boisdinghem	22/04/1918	30/04/1918
War Diary	Seninghem Map Reference	01/05/1918	02/05/1918
War Diary	Hazebrouck 5A-A4	03/05/1918	04/05/1918
War Diary	St. Momelin. Map. Ref. Hazebrouck Sa-(D) 3	05/05/1918	05/05/1918
War Diary	St. Momelin.	06/05/1918	11/05/1918
War Diary	Le. Tom Sheet 27 1.33.c.3.3.	12/05/1918	18/05/1918
War Diary	Le. Tom.	19/05/1918	31/05/1918
War Diary	Le. Tom. Sheet 27-H36d.	01/06/1918	16/06/1918
War Diary	St. Momelin Map Hazebrouck 5A-(D)3	17/06/1918	23/06/1918
War Diary	Lynde. Sheet 36A C11a64	25/06/1918	30/06/1918
War Diary	Lynde Map Reference Sheet 36A B.11.a.6.4.	01/07/1918	14/07/1918
War Diary	Lynde	15/07/1918	31/07/1918
War Diary	Lynde Sheet. 36A-B.11.a.6.4.	01/08/1918	16/08/1918
War Diary	Lynde.	17/08/1918	24/08/1918
War Diary	St. Leger 3CA-C.2.e.3.3.	25/08/1918	29/08/1918
War Diary	St. Leger	30/08/1918	30/08/1918
War Diary	U.30.b.2.2.	31/08/1918	31/08/1918
War Diary	Sheet27 V30b.2.2	01/09/1918	04/09/1918
War Diary	Sheet 36A E11a 24	05/09/1918	30/09/1918
War Diary	Le Paradis Sheet 36 E. 11.924	01/10/1918	04/10/1918
War Diary	Steenwerck. 36A B,30b2.8	05/10/1918	17/10/1918
War Diary	Armentieres.	18/10/1918	20/10/1918
War Diary	Wambrechies. 36. K.2 Central	21/10/1918	27/10/1918
War Diary	Roubaix.	28/10/1918	31/10/1918
War Diary	Tourcoing Sheet 36 F17 Central	01/11/1918	09/11/1918
War Diary	Tourcoing.	10/11/1918	21/11/1918
War Diary	Croix	22/11/1918	30/11/1918
War Diary	Croix Sheet 36 L4d47.	01/12/1918	13/12/1918
War Diary	Croix	14/12/1918	31/12/1918
War Diary	Croix Sheet-36 L4d.4.7	01/01/1919	31/01/1919
War Diary	Croix Sheet 36 L40/47	01/02/1919	28/02/1919

War Diary   51st Mobile Veterinary Section. Broix.   01/03/1919 31/03/1919

WO95/2603/2
51 Mobile Veterinary Section

40TH DIVISION

51ST MOBILE VETY SECTION
JUN 1916-MAR 1919

SIMVets
Vol 1
first

WAR DIARY
or
INTELLIGENCE SUMMARY
(Erase heading not required.)

Army Form C. 2118

Instructions regarding War Diaries and Intelligence Summaries are contained in F.S. Regs., Part II. and the Staff Manual respectively. Title Pages will be prepared in manuscript.

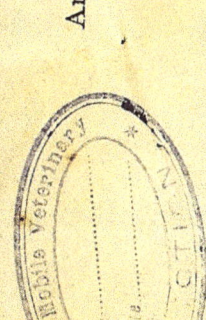

Place	Date	Hour	Summary of Events and Information	Remarks and references to Appendices
DEEPCUT	4/6/16	5.30 AM	Left sick lines at SOUTH MINDEN BARRACKS. DEEPCUT. where had been in training for over 5 months with remainder of 40th Division. marched to FARNBOROUGH. L.I.S.W. Railway Station. Entrained by train starting at 8.10 AM. for SOUTHAMPTON DOCKS. (Half of C.188 R.F.A. were conveyed in same train).	
SOUTHAMPTON.	4/6/16	9.55	Arrived SOUTHAMPTON. Changed 100 horses which had previously been injured. Entrained on to transport ship NORTH WESTERN MILLER which started sailing at 4.30 P.M. Very rough passage.	
HAVRE.	5/6/16	2.30 PM	Arrived HAVRE. disembarked. Ordered to proceed to C. REST CAMP where arrived at about 6 P.M. Interpreter joined. Andre St Vite. Received orders from Camp Commandant re entraining following morning.	
HAVRE.	6/6/16	3.30 AM	Ration party sent forward and main body started at 4 am arriving at Point 3 Gare de Marchandises. Entrained with 40th Divisional Cavalry & 40th Divisional Sanitary Sections and arrived at HILLERS at 2 am. Train travelled via ROUEN and ABBEVILLE, and arrived at 4.30 AM.	
HILLERS.	7/6/16	2 AM.	Received orders from Staff Captain Jones Infantry Brigade to take Section to AMETTES.	
AMETTES.	7/6/16	5 AM.	into area allotted to 40th Divisional Artillery. Artillery Staff Captain later showed exact location of Billets.	
AMETTES.	8/6/16		Rode over to Headquarters 40th Division and received instructions from A.D.V.S. to bring Section nearer Headquarters Division. Visited LAGOULE. FONTES and ST HILAIRE in search of suitable billet and reported to A.D.V.S. on suitability of these places.	
AMETTES	9/6/16		Received orders from A.D.V.S. 40th Division to move Section to LA GOULEE	

WAR DIARY or INTELLIGENCE SUMMARY

Army Form C. 2118

Place	Date	Hour	Summary of Events and Information	Remarks and references to Appendices
AMETTES LA GOULEE.	10/6/16	9 am	Moved section to LA GOULEE. N 30 D 5.7 arriving at 11 am. One section Horse which had contracted Pneumonia in transage overseas left at AMETTES and died later in the day. Arranged for disposal of horse left behind by 18" Welsh with broken leg.	
LA GOULEE	11/6/16		Got into touch with R.V.O. and KILLERS and also with O.C. 23rd M.V.S. (12th Division) at the same place & obtained information re renewal procedure in evacuating horses to Base Hospitals. Orders from A.D.V.S. re collecting horses for the following day.	
LA GOULEE	12/6/16		Rode out with a party consisting of 6 orderlies & men to area occupied by 40th Div Artillery (that is around road from FONTAINE LES HERMANS & AMES) to collect sick horses some of which had been reported left behind by units. Two found dead on arrival & disposed of. Brought 9 back to section.	
LA GOULEE	13/6/16		The Interpreter leaves Unit. Posted to 13th Yorks Pioneers and not allowed for M.V.S.	
LA GOULEE	14/6/16		Rode out with collecting party through to back yard animals left with inhabitants in area occupied by 40th Div. Artillery including two float cases. 9 boat borrowed from 23rd M.V.S. Drew back an implement from field Cashier at KILLERS & paid out men.	
LA GOULEE	15/6/16		Advised by A.D.V.S. to send a party forward to billets occupied by 23rd M.V.S at KILLERS & take over their billets as we were likely to march there. Left Lynch & 2 men detailed for this. A number of horses about 20 were admitted into 23rd M.V.S. hereon their departure following day & promised to evacuate them to Base Hospital for this Unit. O.C. interviewed by D.D.V.S. 1st Army to know whether desirous of holding appointment at R.V. College, London.	

Army Form C. 2118

WAR DIARY
or
INTELLIGENCE SUMMARY
(Erase heading not required.)

Instructions regarding War Diaries and Intelligence Summaries are contained in F.S. Regs., Part II. and the Staff Manual respectively. Title Pages will be prepared in manuscript.

Place	Date	Hour	Summary of Events and Information	Remarks and references to Appendices
LA GOULEE	16/6/16		Brought in remounts from no.1 Field Remount Depot at GONNEHEM for distribution to 40th Divisional Troops according to instructions from D.A.Q.M.G. Arranged with R.V.O. at LILLERS for trucks for evacuation of horses tomorrow. Obtained decree orders from General Staff 40th Division to move Section on 19th to BRUAY (that being area allotted for concentration of 40th Division).	
LA GOULEE	17/6/16		45 sick animals despatched by train from LILLERS to Veterinary Hospital NEUFCHATEL. Corpl Elliott & 5 men in charge. 30 of these were lifted by 23rd M.V.S. 12th Division, remainder by A.H.Q. & remainder from 40th Division. Train started at 4.47 p.m. Billeting party brought back from LILLERS & received orders to send a billeting party forward to BRUAY tomorrow morning. 2 Horses destroyed namely 1 brought into section & 1 left by 18th Welsh at ST HILAIRE, taken by horse slaughterer at LILLERS. £220 francs received from him.	
LA GOULEE	18/6/16		Wired to R.V.O. LILLERS instructions for return of conducting party. Sergt Brown & 2 men sent forward at 5 a.m. to BRUAY as billeting party.	
LA GOULEE BRUAY	19/6/16	6 a.m.	Section moved to BRUAY arrived at 10 a.m. Position of horse lines RUE DE LA PLACE DU BRUAY. J10A6.9. Yard previously occupied by other M.V.S. prior to that by French troops. Men placed in straw sheds. Horse accommodation very good.	
BRUAY	20/6/16			
BRUAY	21/6/16		Conducting party sent to NEUFCHATEL now returned. Taken by A.D.V.S. in 1 car in block for horses to left behind by 40th Division namely 1 left at LES PESSES by 294 Coy A.S.C., 1 by 13th Yorks at HAM EN ARTOIS (These two to be destroyed. 1 left at CHOCQUES found to be already destroyed, 1 left by 40 Sig Coy R.E. at NORRENT FONTES to be collected & brought into Section.)	

WAR DIARY or INTELLIGENCE SUMMARY

Army Form C. 2118

Place	Date	Hour	Summary of Events and Information	Remarks and references to Appendices
BRUAY.	22/6/16		N.C.O. & man sent out to bring in above horse. He collected & took out myself & hand horse recovery from no 2 to inhabitants for above horses + two that horses for slaughter had been disposed of. Received 220 frcs for 2 carcases. 6.30 P.M. received through A.D.V.S. copy of orders from D.V.S. to report to Principal R.V. College, London forthwith.	
BRUAY	23/6/16		One horse from H.Q. Div. Signal Coy suspected mange and from same unit Debility x 2 from 135 Field Ambulance admitted.	
BRUAY.	24/6/16		Arranged with A.D.V.S. to dress horses of Signal Coy. H.Q. which had been in contact with mange case. Went to DIVISION to collect 2 horses according to orders received from 19 D.V.S. 1st Army, which had been left by 23rd Division. I arranged to be destroyed. I brought back + brought in another abandoned by some unit unknown.	
BRUAY	25/6/16		Handed over temporarily 51st M.V.S. to Lieut. V. de Boisoere. A.V.C. vol/c H.Q. Divisional Train, pending arrival of Capt. Q.C. Lancaster A.V.C. to take over unit permanently.	

In the Field
25/6/16

J.W. Edward Clifford?
J.W. S.M.R.V.S.

WAR DIARY or INTELLIGENCE SUMMARY

Army Form C. 2118

Place	Date	Hour	Summary of Events and Information	Remarks and references to Appendices
BRUAY.	26/6/16	6 AM.	Capt G.Y. Edwards left the Unit for England. 1 Skin & 8 other sick animals evacuated from CHOCQUES to Base Veterinary Hospital at NEUF CHATEL. Sold 1 horse to Mons. Vanut. BRUAY horse slaughterer and received 100 francs for same. Capt. G. C. Lancaster arrived in evening.	
BRUAY	27/6/16	9 AM.	Capt G. C. Lancaster officially took over 51st M.V.S from Lieut de Loraine A.V.C. On inspection was made of men equipment & horses. all was found correct.	
BRUAY.	28/6/16		Colonel. E. E. Martin C.M.G. D.D.V.S. 1st Army. inspected 51st M.V.S at 3 p.m. Pte E Ranton reported himself for duty from No 6 C.C.S. at Corps McLaughlin A.J. reported himself for duty with 51st M.V.S from H.Q. 40th Division. Conducting party sent to NEUFCHATEL on 26/6/16. returned.	
BRUAY.	29/6/16		Received 2 horses for evacuation from No1 Coy A.V.C. Received notification that Railhead would be at Lillers in future.	
BRUAY.	30/6/16		2/Section & quick horses mallined. 6 animals admitted.	

Lillefield
30/6/16

G L Lancaster Capt A.V.C
A.V.S
COMMANDING 51st MOBILE VETN. SECTION.
HQ Division

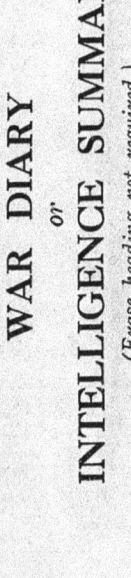

Wm Dean /
Capt. L.C Lancade AVC
O.C 51 M.V.S. No Div
from Jan 1 — Jan 31. 1906

40 July
51 MVS
Vet

Army Form C. 2118

WAR DIARY
or
INTELLIGENCE SUMMARY
(Erase heading not required.)

Instructions regarding War Diaries and Intelligence Summaries are contained in F. S. Regs., Part II. and the Staff Manual respectively. Title Pages will be prepared in manuscript.

Place	Date	Hour	Summary of Events and Information	Remarks and references to Appendices
BRUAY	1/7/16	9.30 a.m.	58 horses of Divisional Hd. Qrs. and 6 of Signal Coy. were malleined; also 46 horses and 29 mules of 229 Coy. R.E. and 4 horses of the Section.	
BRUAY	1/7/16	12.30 p.m.	Arrangements were made with the R.T.O., BRUAY, to evacuate 12 horses to-morrow.	
BRUAY	2/7/16	12 noon	1 skin and 11 other cases were evacuated to NEUFCHATEL. Corpl. Elliott was in charge of the conducting party. 8 horses of the 136th Field Ambulance and 3 of 229th Coy. R.E. were malleined.	
BRUAY	3/7/16	10 a.m.	1 mule from 40th Signal Coy. R.E. was admitted as reactor to mallein.	
BRUAY	3/7/16	2.30 p.m.	The above mule was inoculated by the A.D.V.S. It was inoculated on the opposite eye and a subcutaneous injection also was given; the maximum temperature recorded was 102.4 at 9 p.m. and the minimum temperature was 99.4 at 6 a.m. on the following morning.	

1875 Wt. W593/826 1,000,000 4/15 J.B.C. & A. A.D.S.S./Forms/C. 2118.

Army Form C. 2118

WAR DIARY
or
INTELLIGENCE SUMMARY
(Erase heading not required.)

Instructions regarding War Diaries and Intelligence Summaries are contained in F.S. Regs., Part II. and the Staff Manual respectively. Title Pages will be prepared in manuscript.

Place	Date	Hour	Summary of Events and Information	Remarks and references to Appendices
BRUAY.	3/7/16	5.30 p.m.	Circular Memo. No. 99 of D.V.S. was received from A.D.V.S. Owing to the large number of injuries shown under class 13 on A.F. A2002, in future, the number of those considered of a preventable nature is to be given, with the letter "P" added.	
DROUVIN	4/7/16	9.30 a.m.	The Section moved by road to DROUVIN (sheet 36 B¼₀,₀₀₀ — K.H.@) reaching there at 10.45 a.m. The billet was taken over from 2nd Mobile Vety. Section, 1st Division. This Section proceeded to occupy billet vacated by us. One injured horse was left at BRUAY and a mange case left by 2nd M.V.S. was taken over at DROUVIN. A wire was sent to R.T.O. BETHUNE asking him to direct	
DROUVIN	4/7/16	11 a.m.	returning party from NEUFCHATEL to report at DROUVIN.	
DROUVIN	5/7/16	9 a.m.	The Conducting Party returned from NEUFCHATEL. A party was detailed to proceed to Noeux-les-mines station to collect 20 remounts for units of the Division. As no representatives of the units were present to receive	

Army Form C. 2118

WAR DIARY
or
INTELLIGENCE SUMMARY
(Erase heading not required.)

Instructions regarding War Diaries and Intelligence Summaries are contained in F.S. Regs., Part II. and the Staff Manual respectively. Title Pages will be prepared in manuscript.

Place	Date	Hour	Summary of Events and Information	Remarks and references to Appendices
DROUVIN	6/7/16		them, the animals were brought back to the Section, and wires were sent to the units informing them to send for the remounts.	
DROUVIN	7/7/16		Admitted 4 animals for Evacuation	
DROUVIN	7/7/16		Corp. McLaughlin and 1 man sent to BRUAY to take charge of Mobile Vety Section-Billets. There units a Mobile Veterinary Section arrived. 120 francs received from Field debassier A.V.C. NO i/c HQ "Dunninial Train" for carcase of Horse.	
DROUVIN	8/7/16		Evacuated 24 animals (sick) to Veterinary Hospital NEUFCHATEL in charge of Corpl. Elliott + 3 men.	
DROUVIN	9/7/16		Corpl. McLaughlin + 1 man returned from BRUAY having handed over Billets &c. to 15" M.V.S. 8" Division.	
DROUVIN	10/7/16		Admitted 22 sick animals. arranged with R. TO NOEUX-LES-MINES for evacuation of 32 animals tomorrow.	
DROUVIN	11/7/16		Admitted 9 animals. 32 animals evacuated to Veterinary Hospital NEUFCHATEL in charge of Corpl. Oliver + 3 men.	
DROUVIN	12/7/16		Admitted 4 sick animals.	
DROUVIN	13/7/16		Conducting party returned from NEUFCHATEL. Admitted 5 sick animals from H.Q. "D.A.C."	

WAR DIARY
or
INTELLIGENCE SUMMARY

(Erase heading not required.)

Army Form C. 2118

Place	Date	Hour	Summary of Events and Information	Remarks and references to Appendices
DROUVIN	14/7/16		Received orders from A.D.V.S. 40th Division to find suitable site for an advanced Receiving Station. I went to RESREBIS and arranged for a suitable place there to be reserved for Mobile Veterinary Section and put up two painted boards showing Veterinary Sign and Divisional mark ◇.	
DROUVIN	15/7/16		Admitted 32 animals. Arranged with R.T.O. NOEUX-LES-MINES for trucks to evacuate 47 animals tomorrow.	
DROUVIN	16/7/16		Evacuated to Base Veterinary Hospital 47 animals in charge of Corpl Burns and 6 men. Admitted 2 animals.	
DROUVIN	17/7/16		Drew 20 remounts from YONNE A.A.M. for Units of 40th Division. Admitted 9 animals.	
DROUVIN	18/7/16		Admitted 12 sick animals. Conducting party sent to Base on 16/7/16 returned. Arranged with R.T.O. NOEUX-LES-MINES for trucks for evacuation of 23 animals tomorrow.	
DROUVIN	19/7/16		S.S. 1 Horse to M. Veton. BETHUNE for distruction. Evacuated to Base Veterinary Hospital 23 animals in charge of Corpl McLaughlin and 2 men. Admitted 10 animals.	
DROUVIN	20/7/16		Admitted 9 sick animals. Arranged for evacuation of 16 animals tomorrow.	
DROUVIN	21/7/16		Drew from NOEUX-LES-MINES station 12 remounts for Units of 40th Division in accordance with orders received from A.D.V.S. 40th Divn. Evacuated to Base Veterinary Hospital 16 animals in charge of Corp. Elliott and 1 man. Admitted 3 animals. Conducting party sent to BASE on 19/7/16 returned.	
DROUVIN	22/7/16		Admitted 4 animals.	
DROUVIN	23/7/16		Conducting party sent on 21st returned. Arranged with R.T.O. NOEUX-LES-MINES for evacuation of 9 animals tomorrow. Admitted 4 sick animals.	

WAR DIARY
or
INTELLIGENCE SUMMARY
(Erase heading not required.)

Army Form C. 2118

Place	Date	Hour	Summary of Events and Information	Remarks and references to Appendices
DROUVIN	24/7/16		Drew 3 remounts from GONNEHAM for 40th Divisional Units. Evacuated to Base Veterinary Hospital 9 animals in charge of Corpl Olivier 1 oneman. Admitted 4 sick animals. In compliance with order received from A.D.V.S. 40th Division Corpl. J. A. Evans sent in charge of one G.S. limbered wagon to ABBEVILLE to draw one Horse Ambulance from No. 5 Veterinary Hospital. The G.S. limbered wagon & horse harness to be left at the Advanced Horse Transport Depot.	
"	25/7/16		Admitted 4 sick animals	
"	26/7/16		Admitted 2 sick animals. Conducting party sent on 24th returned.	
"	27/7/16		Admitted 10 sick animals. Arranged with R.T.O. NOEUX-LES-MINES for evacuation to Base of 19 sick animals.	
"	28/7/16		Admitted 16 sick animals. Evacuated to Base Veterinary Hospital 21 sick animals in charge of Corpl Elliott and 2 men. Drew 5 remounts from Railhead for units of 40th Division.	
"	29/7/16		Admitted 13 animals. Arranged with R.T.O. NOEUX-LES-MINES to evacuate 22 sick animals tomorrow. Corpl. J. A. Evans returned from ABBEVILLE with Horse Ambulance.	
"	30/7/16		Evacuated to Base Veterinary Hospital 22 sick animals in charge of Corpl McLaughlin and 3 men.	
"	31/7/16		Admitted 8 sick animals. Drew 2 H.D. Remounts from GONNEHAM for units of 40th Division.	

W. Rumfin
A.D.V.S. 41st?

G. Lancaster Capt. A.V.C.
O.C. 51st M.V.S. 40th Div.

Army Form C. 2118

WAR DIARY
or
INTELLIGENCE SUMMARY
(Erase heading not required.)

Instructions regarding War Diaries and Intelligence Summaries are contained in F.S. Regs., Part II. and the Staff Manual respectively. Title Pages will be prepared in manuscript.

Place	Date	Hour	Summary of Events and Information	Remarks and references to Appendices
DROUVIN	13/8/16		Evacuated 15 sick animals to base Veterinary Hospital in charge of Corpl Elliott and 2 men.	
	14/8/16		Pte Nuttall No SS 29115 reported for duty with 51st M V.S. from No 9 Veterinary Hospital. Was taken on Strength. At 2.30 P.M. a 9 & limbered wagon with Dvr Wharfe A.S.C. riding the horses + No 6048 Pte J H Simmons riding in wagon left 51st M.V.S. Whereas to fuel dump, got a load of coal. Outside the yard gate 51st M.V.S. the horses bolted & Pte Simmons was thrown from limber sustained a fracture of leg. was removed to No 111 Field Ambulance.	
	15/8/16		Admitted 4 sick animals. Conducting party sent on 13 Aug returned.	
	16/8/16		Admitted 8 animals.	
	17/8/16		Drew from RAILHEAD 28 Remounts for units of 40th Division. admitted 7 animals.	
	18/8/16		Admitted 2 animals. Arranged for evacuation of 15 animals to base tomorrow.	
	19/8/16		Evacuated 16 animals to base Veterinary Hospital in charge of Corpl McLaughlin + one man.	
	20/8/16		Admitted 2 sick animals.	
	21/8/16		Admitted 6 sick animals. Conducting party sent on 19 inst returned.	
	22/8/16		Drew from Railhead 11 Remounts for Units of 40th Division. Admitted 3 animals. Arranged with A.D.V.S. 8th Division for evacuation of 21 sick animals by barge from BETHUNE, on Thursday. Arranged for evacuation of 2 skin cases with R.Vo. NOEUX-LES-MINES	

Army Form C. 2118

WAR DIARY
or
INTELLIGENCE SUMMARY
(Erase heading not required.)

Instructions regarding War Diaries and Intelligence Summaries are contained in F.S. Regs., Part II. and the Staff Manual respectively. Title Pages will be prepared in manuscript.

Place	Date	Hour	Summary of Events and Information	Remarks and references to Appendices
DROUVIN	23/8/16		Evacuated 24 sick animals to Base Veterinary Hospitals by rail in charge of Pte Gates. Sold one horse to 7th Sand BRUAY for destruction & for which received 145fr.o. Admitted 11 animals.	
—	24/8/16		Evacuated 21 sick animals to Base by barge from BETHUNE in charge of Pte Borrows. Sold one horse to 6th NO Staat. BRUAY for destruction. 145fr. received.	
—	25/8/16		Conducting Parties and on 23rd & 24th returned. No 38 1043 Pte Y. Playford reported for duty with 51st M.V.S. from hq Veterinary Hospital vis taken on strength. Admitted 3 sick animals.	
—	26/8/16		Admitted 1 animal.	
—	27/8/16		—	
—	28/8/16		Admitted 2 sick animals. Arranged will A.D.V.S. 8th Division for evacuation of 9 animals by barge tomorrow.	
—	29/8/16		Evacuated to Veterinary Hospitals St OMER 9 animals from BETHUNE by Barge.	
—	30/8/16		Admitted 50 sick animals. Arranged to evacuate 24 by barge from BETHUNE tomorrow.	
—	31/8/16		Evacuated by barge from BETHUNE 24 sick animals in charge of Cooper & Maughlin and one man.	

WWR

G. Lancaster Capt. A.V.C.
COMMANDING 51st MOBILE VETN. SECTION.

Army Form C. 2118

Vol 4 Sheet 1

WAR DIARY or INTELLIGENCE SUMMARY

(Erase heading not required.)

51st Mobile Vety. Sect.
40th Division.

Instructions regarding War Diaries and Intelligence Summaries are contained in F.S. Regs., Part II. and the Staff Manual respectively. Title Pages will be prepared in manuscript.

No. 51 Mobile Veterinary Section

Place	Date	Hour	Summary of Events and Information	Remarks and references to Appendices
DROUVIN Reference Map 36 B K.H.C.	1/9/16		5 sick animals were admitted and arrangements made to evacuate 25 animals from BETHUNE (Map 36 B. E.10 and 11) by barge.	
	2/9/16	8 a.m.	25 sick animals were evacuated to ST.OMER (Map 5A ⓒ 15'③ 45') in charge of Pte. Madden. 1 animal was admitted and the conducting party sent on August 31 at returned.	
	3/9/16		Pte. Madden reported back from ST. OMER and 2 sick animals were admitted.	
	4/9/16		Arrangements were made with the R.T.O. NOEUX-LES-MINES (Map 36 B. L.13) to evacuate 17 sick animals. 9 sick animals were admitted to-day.	
	5/9/16	12:30 a.m.	Despatched 17 animals from NOEUX-LES-MINES to NEUFCHATEL (BOULOGNE) by rail, in charge of Corporal Elliott. During the shunting of the wagons one animal suffering from kick off hind tibia fell and broke the injured leg. The R.T.O. sent for the nearest veterinary officer and had the animal shot.	
	6/9/16		10 sick animals were admitted to-day.	
	7/9/16		The A.D.V.S., 8th Division was notified by wire that this Section had 16 animals for evacuation.	
	8/9/16	8 a.m.	16 animals were evacuated by barge to ST.OMER. 1 skin case was evacuated by rail to NEUFCHATEL in charge of Pte. Carter, conducting party to ST. OMER reported back and 4 animals were admitted.	
	9/9/16	12:30	Great police were received for bales, and also handles for wind screens for horses. An R.E. officer inspected the men's billets to suggest improvements for winter.	
	10/9/16		The A.D.V.S. inspected animals for evacuation and arrangements were made to send them by barge. 6 animals were admitted to-day.	
	11/9/16		1 sick animal was admitted to-day.	

Army Form C. 2118

SHEET NO. 11

WAR DIARY
or
INTELLIGENCE SUMMARY
(Erase heading not required.)

51 M.V.S. 4th Div.

Place	Date	Hour	Summary of Events and Information	Remarks and references to Appendices
DROUVIN	12/9/16	8 a.m.	10 animals were evacuated to ST.OMER by barge. 3 animals were admitted to-day.	
	13/9/16		The A.D.V.S. (Major Rowston) inspected animals for evacuation and 18 animals were admitted. Work is proceeding in preparation for winter campaign. Walls are being improved, concrete floors laid and horse standings made dry. Red chalk for this is being obtained daily from mines at Noeux-LES-MINES.	
	14/9/16	8 a.m.	18 animals were evacuated by barge to ST.OMER, Corporal Oliver being in charge. 1 animal was admitted to-day.	
	15/9/16		1 sick animal was admitted to-day.	
	16/9/16		3 sick animals were admitted.	
	17/9/16		7 " " " "	
	18/9/16		The A.D.V.S. inspected animals for evacuation and arrangements were made to send 7 by rail to NEUFCHATEL. 1 animal was admitted.	
	19/9/16	12.30	7 animals were despatched to NEUFCHATEL, Corporal Evans being in charge. In accordance with instructions received from A.D.V.S., this N.C.O. was ordered to report to O.C. No.12 Veterinary Hospital for instruction in use of the Stewart clipping machine.	
	20/9/16		A.D.V.S. inspected animals for evacuation. General Routine Order No.1810	

Army Form C. 2118

SHEET III

WAR DIARY
or
INTELLIGENCE SUMMARY
(Erase heading not required.)

Instructions regarding War Diaries and Intelligence Summaries are contained in F.S. Regs., Part II. and the Staff Manual respectively. Title Pages will be prepared in manuscript.

51 Mobile Veterinary Section

5/21 M.V.S. 40th Divn

Summary of Events and Information

Place	Date	Hour	Summary of Events and Information	Remarks and references to Appendices
DROUVIN	20/9/16		received from A.D.V.S. Any stray or captured animals of Division are to be sent to the Section. Sick or skin cases to be evacuated. Fit animals to be disposed of according to instructions of D.D.R., 1st Army. Weekly Return of such animals to go to A.D.V.S. Admitted 14 animals to-day.	
	21/9/16 9am.		17 animals were evacuated to ST. OMER by barge from BETHUNE, corporal Elliott being in charge. Corporal Evans reported back from No.12 Veterinary Hospital. 5 animals were admitted to-day including 1 stray one.	
	22/9/16		As 3rd Division was moving arrangements were made for the sick animals of Mobile Section (11th) of that Division to be evacuated by this Section. Orders were received from A.D.V.S. to admit temporarily 1 G.S. Wagon with dynamos, 2 horses and 2 men. This wagon is fitted with catches at back and electric magnets and is used for picking up nails.	
	23/9/16 12.30.		9 animals and 1 H (including 1 skin case) of 3rd DIVISION were evacuated to NEUFCHATEL by rail. One of the horses of this section was too bad to travel and had to return in float. Corporal Phillips was in charge. 2 animals were admitted to-day.	

1875 Wt. W593/826 1,000,000 4/15 J.B.C. & A. A.D.S.S./Forms/C. 2118.

Army Form C. 2118

SHEET IV

WAR DIARY
or
INTELLIGENCE SUMMARY
(Erase heading not required.)

Instructions regarding War Diaries and Intelligence Summaries are contained in F.S. Regs., Part II. and the Staff Manual respectively. Title Pages will be prepared in manuscript.

5101 m V.S. 40 m Divn

Place	Date	Hour	Summary of Events and Information	Remarks and references to Appendices
DROUVIN	24/9/16	9.30	Mine were received from A.D.V.S. to draw 22 Remounts from No.1 Field Remount Depot, GONNEHEM (Map 5ª. G.6.). Units were urged to collect Remounts from the Section	
"	24/9/16	11.30 a.m.	22 Remounts were drawn.	
GONNEHEM	24/9/16			
DROUVIN	24/9/16		3 sick animals were admitted to-day.	
"	25/9/16		O.C. the Section went to LES BREBIS (Map 36.B L.29 a.4.8) to inspect site for advanced collecting station. 5 sick animals were admitted to-day.	
"	26/9/16	9.15 a.m.	Corporal Evans and Pte. Hale were sent to clean up site for advanced collecting station	
		11 a.m.	The A.D.V.S. inspected the billets which are now complete; also sick animals. 17 sick animals were admitted to-day.	
"	27/9/16	3 p.m.	The A.D.V.S. inspected animals for evacuation. Some were ordered to be returned in Section for treatment and back to unit.	
"	28/9/16	8 a.m.	20 animals were evacuated by barge to ST. OMER, Corporal Evans being in charge. 1 animal was admitted.	
"	29/9/16		500 (five hundred) francs) were paid to Field Cashier, 1st Corps for sale of canvas. 8 animals were admitted to-day.	
	30/9/16	2 p.m.	An overhauling of equipment and men's kits took place and practice in packing limber & float. This was a "speed" practice in case of a quick move. Men paraded saddled up. — G. Lancaster (?)	

END

1875 Wt. W593/826 1,000,000 4/15 J.B.C. & A. A.D.S.S./Forms/C. 2118.

Army Form C. 2118

Vol 5

WAR DIARY
or
INTELLIGENCE SUMMARY
(Erase heading not required.)

No. 51 Mobile Veterinary Section
No.
Date 3/10/16

Place	Date	Hour	Summary of Events and Information	Remarks and references to Appendices
DROUVIN	1/10/16		Eight animals were admitted to-day and three spare remounts were issued to 178th Bde, R.F.A.	
do.	2/10/16		The A.D.V.S. inspected animals for evacuation. One animal admitted yesterday died of tetanus.	
do.	3/10/16	8 a.m.	Twenty animals were evacuated by barge from BETHUNE to ST. OMER, and 2 animals were admitted	
do.	4/10/16	2.30 p.m.	The A.D.V.S. inspected animals for evacuation and arrangements were made to evacuate 14 from BETHUNE. Eleven sick animals were admitted.	
do.	5/10/16	8 a.m.	Fourteen animals were evacuated by barge from BETHUNE to ST. OMER, Corporal Elliott being in charge. Two animals were admitted.	
do.	6/10/16		A wire was received to draw 16 remounts from GONNEHEM on following day. No animals were admitted to-day.	
do.	7/10/16		The 16 remounts were drawn from No.1 Field Remount Depot and issued to units the same day. Three sick animals were admitted.	
do.	8/10/16		Stores were received to-day from No.1 Advanced Base of Veterinary Stores and a wire was received to draw remounts on the following day.	

Army Form C. 2118

WAR DIARY
or
INTELLIGENCE SUMMARY
(Erase heading not required.)

Instructions regarding War Diaries and Intelligence Summaries are contained in F.S. Regs., Part II. and the Staff Manual respectively. Title Pages will be prepared in manuscript.

Place	Date	Hour	Summary of Events and Information	Remarks and references to Appendices
DROUVIN	9/10/16		Nine Remounts were drawn from GONNEHEM and issued to units and 6 animals were admitted.	
do.	10/10/16		Eighteen animals were evacuated by barge from BETHUNE to ST. OMER.	
do.	11/10/16		Seven sick animals were admitted to-day.	
do.	12/10/16		Admitted 1 stray mule found on LENS-PHILOSOPHE Road. This animal was advertised in Divisional Routine Orders.	
do.	13/10/16		S/Cpl. Robertson, 120th Machine Gun Company reported here for instruction in the use of the Stewart Clipping Machine. As all accommodation on the barge was taken up arrangements were made to evacuate by rail. The mule (stray) was claimed by the 20th Middlesex Regt. During the absence of A.D.V.S. (Major Rowstron) in England, Captain Lancaster acted for him.	
do.	14/10/16		Eighteen animals were evacuated by rail from NOEUX-LES-MINES to NEUFCHATEL. PTE Barefoot of this Section reported to Headquarters Coy., 40th Divisional Train, to undergo a test as a cold shoer. The clipping of animals is now in progress. Eight animals were admitted.	

WAR DIARY or INTELLIGENCE SUMMARY

Army Form C. 2118

Place	Date	Hour	Summary of Events and Information	Remarks and references to Appendices
DROUVIN	15/10/16		A wire was received to draw 11 remounts from GONNEHEM. These were drawn and issued to units. Two animals were admitted. Pte. Playford of the Section left for leave to England.	
do.	16/10/16		L.Corpl. Robertson having undergone his instruction clipping, reported back to his unit.	
do.	17/10/16	12.30 pm	One skin case (Dvr. Stonnell, A.S.C. L/2) was sent by rail to NEUFCHATEL. Four sick animals were admitted.	
do.	18/10/16		Eight animals were admitted and arrangements made to evacuate from BETHUNE.	
do.	19/10/16	7am	Twenty three animals were evacuated by barge from BETHUNE to ST.OMER including 2 mules cast by D.D.R., 1st Army, as unmanageable. One of these broke away on the march & could not be caught in time for the barge.	
do.	20/10/16		Eleven animals were admitted including 1 stray sent by A.P.M., 1st Corps. The senior sergeant of 36th Mobile Vet. Section came to see billets for the in-coming Mobile Section.	
do.	21/10/16		Seven animals were evacuated by barge from BETHUNE to ST.OMER. The O.C. of the Section was instructed to evacuate by rail every day to keep Section clear in case of a move. Thirteen animals were admitted.	

Army Form C. 2118

WAR DIARY
or
INTELLIGENCE SUMMARY
(Erase heading not required.)

Instructions regarding War Diaries and Intelligence Summaries are contained in F. S. Regs., Part II. and the Staff Manual respectively. Title Pages will be prepared in manuscript.

Place	Date	Hour	Summary of Events and Information	Remarks and references to Appendices
DROUVIN	21/10/16	8.30 a.m.	Notice was received to be at Railhead at 11.30 a.m. to receive 40 remounts. Thirty of these were to be issued and 10 kept in reserve. Thirty-nine were received, twenty-nine issued and remainder kept in reserve.	
do.	22/10/16		Fifteen sick animals (including 1 skin case) were evacuated by rail from NOEUX-LES-MINES to NEUFCHATEL. Corpl. Evans being in charge.	
do.	23/10/16		Two Remount cases were evacuated to No.1 Field Remount Depot, GONNEHEM, by order of D.D.R., 1st Army. Eight animals were admitted.	
do.	24/10/16		The A.D.V.S. inspected animals for evacuation. Pte. Playford reported back from leave from England. Copy of name sent by A.D.V.S. to A.D.V.S, 24th Division, saying Mobile Section (36th) of that Division would take over of 29th inst. and occupy on the 30th.	
do	25/10/16		Fifteen animals were evacuated by rail from NOEUX-LES-MINES to NEUFCHATEL. Capt. Lowry, O.C. 36th M.V.S, inspected billets for incoming M.V.S.	
do	26/10/16		The A.D.V.S. inspected animals for evacuation. A wire was received to draw and issue 11 remounts from GONNEHEM. Animals were admitted.	
do	27/10/16		Eleven animals were evacuated by rail to NEUFCHATEL.	

No. 51 Mobile Veterinary 31/10/16

Army Form C. 2118

WAR DIARY
or
INTELLIGENCE SUMMARY
(Erase heading not required.)

Instructions regarding War Diaries and Intelligence Summaries are contained in F.S. Regs., Part II. and the Staff Manual respectively. Title Pages will be prepared in manuscript.

Place	Date	Hour	Summary of Events and Information	Remarks and references to Appendices
DROUVIN.	28/10/16		Four sick animals were admitted.	
do.	29/10/16		Corporal from 36th Mobile Veterinary Section reported to take over from us. Thirteen sick animals were handed over to his section.	
do.	30/10/16		The Section left DROUVIN at 8 a.m. — comprising 1 Officer, 2 N.C.Os and men A.V.C., 2 A.S.C. drivers attached and 1 G.S. wagon (supply) and donkey. The Section proceeded by road to ROLLECOURT via BRUAY and ST. POL, which was reached at 4 p.m.	
do.	31/10/16	8.30 am	Supplies were drawn for 1/11/12.	
		4.00 pm	Supplies were drawn for 2/11/12.	

N° 51 Mobile Veterinary Section 31/10/16

G. N. Lancaster Capt. A.V.C.
COMMANDING 51ST MOBILE VETN. SECTION.

ROLLECOURT,
ARRAS ROAD
ST. POL.
SECTION □
END.

WAR DIARY
or
INTELLIGENCE SUMMARY

(Erase heading not required.)

Army Form C. 2118

Mob Vety Sec

VI 26

Place	Date	Hour	Summary of Events and Information	Remarks and references to Appendices
ROELLECOURT	1/11/16	11am	One officer's charger, under treatment, was discharged to the 12th Suffolk Regt.	
		3pm	Orders were received from A.D.V.S. to stand by in readiness for a move. The float was sent to CHELERS, 7 miles east of ST. POL. to fetch a horse	
do.	2/11/16		The O.C. spent the day in locating units	
do.	3/11/16	6pm	Orders were received to proceed to FROHEN-LE-GRAND in 1 days march.	
do.	4/11/16	8.30 am	The Section set out from ROELLE COURT at 8.30am. One sick animal, unable to travel was left in charge of a farmer. The journey was via ST.POL, FREVENT and FROHEN-LE-GRAND was reached at 4.30pm. As no billets were available in FROHEN-LE-PETIT, the Section billeted in FROHEN-LE-PETIT. Orders were received to proceed on the following day to BERNAVILLE.	
FROHEN-LE-PETIT	5/11/16	9.30 am	The Section set out for BERNAVILLE which was reached at 11.30 a.m.. Two sick animals were collected en route.	
do	6/11/16		Orders were received to transfer No. S.E. 12794 Pte. Farrell, A.V.C. to Cavalry Reinforcements Base Depot, ROUEN,	

Army Form C. 2118

WAR DIARY
or
INTELLIGENCE SUMMARY
(Erase heading not required.)

Instructions regarding War Diaries and Intelligence Summaries are contained in F. S. Regs., Part II. and the Staff Manual respectively. Title Pages will be prepared in manuscript.

Place	Date	Hour	Summary of Events and Information	Remarks and references to Appendices
BERNAVILLE	7/11/16	7am	No.S.E. 1279A, Pte. Yarrell A.V.C. left Railhead for the Base. The O.C. spent the day with the A.D.V.S. locating animals for collection.	
do.	8/11/16		Six animals were collected.	
do.	9/11/16		Three animals were collected.	
do.	10/11/16	2.30 pm	The A.D.V.S. inspected animals for evacuation. 16 animals were evacuated from CONTEVILLE to ABBEVILLE. One animal was collected at PROUVILLE.	
do.	11/11/16		One horse was collected from No.12 Prisoners of War Company.	
do.	12/11/16		One animal was collected from RIBEAUCOURT.	
do.	13/11/16		Two men of Section (Pte. Madden & Pte. Roberts) reported to 137th Field Ambulance for dental treatment.	
do.	14/11/16		Admitted 1 horse. The D.D.V.S. 5th Army and the A.D.V.S. visited the Section. An A.V.C. Sergeant with high strength taken on the strength prior to his posting to a unit.	

Army Form C. 2118

WAR DIARY
or
INTELLIGENCE SUMMARY
(Erase heading not required.)

Instructions regarding War Diaries and Intelligence Summaries are contained in F. S. Regs., Part II. and the Staff Manual respectively. Title Pages will be prepared in manuscript.

Place	Date	Hour	Summary of Events and Information	Remarks and references to Appendices
BERNAVILLE	15/11/16	6.30 a.m.	The Section was ordered to proceed from BERNAVILLE to FROHEN-LE-GRAND by road and reached the latter place at 1 p.m.	
FROHEN-LE-GRAND PETIT.	16/11/16		The A.D.V.S. visited the section to give O.C. the list of units billets. 5 animals (including 1 skin case) were evacuated from CONTEVILLE to ABBEVILLE. The A.V.C. Sergeant attached to the Section was ordered to report to the 122nd H. Battery, 2nd H.A.G. He left VAIX-LE-CHATEAU at 2 p.m.	
do.	17/11/16		The Section was ordered to hold itself in readiness for a move.	
do.	18/11/16	Show.	Orders were received to proceed by road to BOUQUE MAISON.	
do.	19/11/16		The Section left at 10 a.m. and reached BOUQUE MAISON at 1.30 p.m.	
BOUQUE-MAISON	20/11/16		No. S.E. 5940 Pte. Barefoot, A.V.C. was charged with "neglect of duty in that on the night of Nov. 18th 1916, when posted as picquet, he left the horse lines to go to an entertainment for drink." He was tried when, and sentenced to 21 days No.1 Field Punishment. Two sick animals were admitted from the 30th Division and 1 from the 7th Division	

WAR DIARY
or
INTELLIGENCE SUMMARY
(Erase heading not required.)

Army Form C. 2118

Place	Date	Hour	Summary of Events and Information	Remarks and references to Appendices
BOUQUE MAISON	20/11/16	11 a.m.	No. S.E. 0715 Pte. Nuttall, A.V.C. left for leave to England.	
do.	21/11/16	3 p.m.	Twelve sick animals were evacuated to ABBEVILLE. Pte. Playford and Pte. Rossit. Orders were received to march to DOULLENS.	
do.	22/11/16		The Section marched to DOULLENS which was reached at 12.30 p.m.	
DOULLENS	23/11/16	10 a.m.	The section set out at 10 a.m. for CANAPLES which was reached at 3.30 p.m.	
CANAPLES	24/11/16	6 a.m.	The Section marched to AILLY-LE-HAUT-CLOCHER via ST. OUEN. One animal was collected at BERTEAUCOURT. Rested at ST. OUEN where one horse was collected. AILLY was reached at 6 p.m. The roads en route were very muddy and sufficient for transport. More suitable billets were secured at FAMECHON.	
AILLY-LE-HAUT-CLOCHER	25/11/16			
FAMECHON	26/11/16		The Section removed by this place. The A.D.V.S. inspected the billets. Prior to his departure for England on leave the O.C. handed over to Capt. V.R. de Roisserre, A.V.C.	G.C. Lancastle Capt.

Army Form C. 2118

WAR DIARY
or
INTELLIGENCE SUMMARY
(Erase heading not required.)

Instructions regarding War Diaries and Intelligence Summaries are contained in F. S. Regs., Part II. and the Staff Manual respectively. Title Pages will be prepared in manuscript.

Place	Date	Hour	Summary of Events and Information	Remarks and references to Appendices
FAMECHON	27/11/16		Capt. W.R. de Boisière, A.V.C. assumed command of the Section. Six sick animals were admitted.	
do	28/11/16		Notice came from A.D.V.S. that sick animals may be evacuated by	
		7pm	road to ABBEVILLE. Orders were received to proceed to ABBEVILLE to draw remounts.	
do	29/11/16	9 a.m.	The O.C. and 15 men proceeded to ABBEVILLE and drew 25 horses and 11 mules remounts. The A.D.V.S. inspected animals for evacuation.	
do	30/11/16	7.45 a.m.	Nine sick animals were evacuated by road to ABBEVILLE, Corporal Elliott being in charge. The conducting party proceeded to Remount Depôt where they were met by Capt. de Boisière and 12 H.D. remounts were drawn.	

END.

WWR

W. R. de Boisière
Capt. A.V.C.

Army Form C. 2118

WAR DIARY
or
INTELLIGENCE SUMMARY
(Erase heading not required.)

Vol 7

No. 51 Mobile Veterinary Section — No. ... Date 31/12/16

Place	Date	Hour	Summary of Events and Information	Remarks and references to Appendices
FAMECHON.	2/12/16		Corporal Elliott was sent to BERTEAUCOURT to collect a stray horse.	
do.	4/12/16		The A.D.V.S. inspected sick animals for evacuation.	
do.	5/12/16	9.30 a.m.	Ten sick animals were evacuated by road to ABBEVILLE.	
do.	6/12/16		No. S.E. 2715 Pte. Nuttall reported back from leave from England. Ten remounts were drawn from Advanced Depot at ABBEVILLE and issued to units.	
do.	7/12/16		One sick animal was admitted.	
do.	8/12/16		No. S.E. 6164 Pte. Hall was admitted to 136th Field Ambulance suffering from influenza. Two sick animals were admitted. A wire was received from 136th Field Ambulance saying Pte. Hall had been evacuated to No. 2 Stationary Hospital.	
do.	9/12/16			
do.	10/12/16		The A.D.V.S. inspected sick animals for evacuation.	
do.	11/12/16		Five sick animals were sent to ABBEVILLE by road, Corpl. Elliott being in charge. A movement order was received from the A.D.V.S.	
do.	12/12/16		Corpl. McLaughlin proceeded to ABBEVILLE in charge of a float case. An urgent movement order was received from the A.D.V.S.	

Army Form C. 2118

WAR DIARY
or
INTELLIGENCE SUMMARY
(Erase heading not required.)

Instructions regarding War Diaries and Intelligence Summaries are contained in F.S. Regs., Part II. and the Staff Manual respectively. Title Pages will be prepared in manuscript.

Place	Date	Hour	Summary of Events and Information	Remarks and references to Appendices
FAMECHON	12/12/16		The Section was ordered to proceed to 15th Corps Middle Area in 2 days' march. No. S.E.11952 Sergt. Brown was admitted to 135th Field Ambulance suffering from diarrhoea.	
do.	13/12/16	9.30 am	The Section marched with the 120th Infantry Brigade Transport to ST. SAUVEUR which was reached at 3.30 p.m. A wire was received saying Sergt. Brown had been evacuated to No.1 South African General Hospital.	
ST. SAUVEUR	13/12/16	7 his am	The Section marched to VAUX-SUR-SOMME via AMIENS which town had to be cleared by 11 am. VAUX was reached at 4 p.m.	
VAUX-SUR-SOMME	15/12/16	10 am	The Section marched to CHIPILLY which was reached at 11 am. The roads were very difficult for transport. Captain Lancaster, returned from leave, met the Section at CORBIE.	
CHIPILLY	16/12/16		Capt. de Borieine left, after handing over to Captain Lancaster. A wire was received from A.D.V.S. to send 1 N.C.O. and 5 men for duty with the 43rd V.M.V.S., 33rd Division.	
do.	17/12/16		Corpl. Elliott and 5 men were conducted by the O.C. to the 43rd M.V.S.	

Army Form C. 2118

WAR DIARY
or
INTELLIGENCE SUMMARY
(Erase heading not required.)

Instructions regarding War Diaries and Intelligence Summaries are contained in F. S. Regs., Part II. and the Staff Manual respectively. Title Pages will be prepared in manuscript.

Place	Date	Hour	Summary of Events and Information	Remarks and references to Appendices
CHIPILLY	18/12/16		to duty.	
do.	19/12/16		2 stray animals were admitted. Four animals were admitted.	
do.	21/12/16		Seven sick animals were evacuated from MERICOURT to FORGES-LES-EAUX. The A.D.V.S. inspected these prior to their departure.	
do.	22/12/16		The O.C. and the A.D.V.S. inspected site for Section at BRAY-	
do.	24/12/16		One stray animal was admitted.	
do.	25/12/16		Pte. Nuttall reported back from FORGES.	
do.	26/12/16		The Section moved from CHIPILLY to BRAY-SUR-SOMME. Some sick animals were taken and Corporal Evans was left in charge of a float case.	
BRAY-SUR-SOMME	27/12/16		Seven sick animals were evacuated from BRAY to FORGES-LES-EAUX. The A.D.V.S. inspected the Section's billet and also the sick animals.	
do.	28/12/16		Six sick animals were admitted.	
do.	29/12/16		Nine sick animals were admitted.	
do.	30/12/16		Twenty sick animals, including three skin cases were	

WAR DIARY
or
INTELLIGENCE SUMMARY

Army Form C. 2118

Place	Date	Hour	Summary of Events and Information	Remarks and references to Appendices
BRAY-SUR-SOMME.			evacuated from BRAY to FORGES. Corporal Elliott being in charge. The men attached to the 43rd M.V.S. reported back and an N.C.O. and four men from the 43rd M.V.S., 33rd Division, reported here for duty.	
do.	31/12/16.		Twenty five sick animals were evacuated from Bray to FORGES-LES-EAUX, Corporal Elliott being in charge.	

G. Carruthers Capt.
A.V.C.
COMMANDING 51st MOBILE VETY. SECTION.

WAR DIARY
or
INTELLIGENCE SUMMARY
(Erase heading not required.)

Army Form C. 2118

Place	Date	Hour	Summary of Events and Information	Remarks and references to Appendices
BRAY-SUR-SOMME	1/1/17		Eleven animals were received and twenty evacuated to FORGES-LES-EAUX. The A.D.V.S. inspected the animals prior to evacuation.	
do.	2/1/17		MARICOURT was selected by the A.D.V.S. as a suitable place for an Advanced Collecting Station. Capt. Lancaster visited this place and chose a billet for this Station.	
do.	3/1/17		Fourteen sick animals were received to-day. An N.C.O. and two men proceeded to MARICOURT to open the Advanced Collecting Station. The place was advertised in Divisional Routine Orders. Twenty-six animals were received and twenty evacuated to FORGES.	
do.	4/1/17		Six animals were received and ten evacuated.	
do.	5/1/17		Ten animals were received and nine evacuated.	
do.	6/1/17		Nineteen animals were received and eight evacuated.	
do.	7/1/17		Fourteen animals were received including seven from the Advanced Station. Twenty-one were evacuated. The A.D.V.S. inspected these before evacuation.	
do.	8/1/17		Twelve animals were received including five from Advanced Station and fourteen were evacuated to FORGES.	
do.	9/1/17		Thirty-five animals were received including thirteen from Advanced Station and twenty-one were evacuated.	
do.	10/1/17		Thirty-eight animals were received and 38 were evacuated to FORGES.	
do.	11/1/17		Twenty-nine animals including 16 from Advanced Station were received and 25 evacuated.	
do.	12/1/17		Thirty-six animals were received including 13 from Advanced Station.	

Army Form C. 2118

WAR DIARY
or
INTELLIGENCE SUMMARY
(Erase heading not required.)

Instructions regarding War Diaries and Intelligence Summaries are contained in F.S. Regs., Part II. and the Staff Manual respectively. Title Pages will be prepared in manuscript.

Place	Date	Hour	Summary of Events and Information	Remarks and references to Appendices
BRAY-SUR-SOMME.	13/1/17		Four of these were retained for treatment and 30 evacuated.	
do.	14/1/17		Twenty one animals were received including 8 from the Advanced Station. There was no evacuation to-day owing to shelling. Twelve animals were received including 6 from Advanced Station and 36 were evacuated. A confidential memo. was received from the A.D.V.S. re congestion in Base Hospitals and measures to be taken to alleviate this.	
do.	15/1/17		Twenty-seven animals were received including from Advanced Station. Two were retained for treatment and 19 evacuated.	
do.	16/1/17		Sixteen animals were received, 6 retained for treatment and 20 evacuated.	
do.	17/1/17		Nine animals were received including 6 from Advanced Station; 2 were retained for treatment and 8 evacuated.	
do.	18/1/17		Seventeen animals were received.	
do.	19/1/17		Six animals were received, 6 retained for treatment and 14 evacuated.	
do.	20/1/17		Twenty-eight animals were received including 11 from Advanced Station. Two animals were retained for treatment and 16 evacuated.	
do.	21/1/17		Twelve animals were received, 2 retained for treatment and 1k evacuated.	
do.	22/1/17		Twenty animals were received and eight evacuated.	
do.	23/1/17		Thirty nine animals were received. Among these were 12 received from No.2, Section, 8th D.A.C. As one of these was found to have Stomatitis, it and the others were ordered by the A.D.V.S. to be returned to the unit. Four animals were retained for treatment and 31 evacuated.	

WAR DIARY
or
INTELLIGENCE SUMMARY
(Erase heading not required.)

Army Form C. 2118

Place	Date	Hour	Summary of Events and Information	Remarks and references to Appendices
BRAY-SUR SOMME	24/1/17		Three animals were received.	
do.	25/1/17		One animal was received and 2 from Advanced Station. Eight animals were evacuated.	
do.	26/1/17		Ten animals were received (9 without wounds).	
do.	27/1/17		One animal was received. The Advanced Collecting Station was closed at 12 noon to-day.	
do.	28/1/17		The Section marched from BRAY to CHIPILLY after handing over kit to the 15th M.V.S., 8th Div. Forty two sick animals under treatment were sent on at 7 a.m. to CHIPILLY. An N.C.O. and 4 men were left in charge and the rest of the conducting party returned to move with the Section. These 4 men are attached from units of the Division to assist in looking after the sick animals under treatment. Fifteen animals were handed over to the O.C. 15th M.V.S. for evacuation. An N.C.O. and 3 men were left with the 15th M.V.S. to assist them in evacuations. A wire was received from the A.D.V.S. to suspend evacuations for the present owing to congestion on the railways.	
do.	29/1/17		Work proceeded in preparing a large barn for the treatment of sick animals.	
do.	30/1/17		Saddles, etc, are being cleaned up, men's clothing etc. inspected, as it was impossible to attend to these things while the Division was in the line.	

WAR DIARY
or
INTELLIGENCE SUMMARY

(Erase heading not required.)

Army Form C. 2118

Place	Date	Hour	Summary of Events and Information	Remarks and references to Appendices
CHIPILLY	1/2/17		The A.D.V.S. inspected animals under treatment and notified O.C. to select horses for discharge as the Division was standing by, to move at 48 hours notice. Four animals were admitted.	
do.	2/2/17		Eight animals were discharged to their units.	
do.	3/2/17		Four animals were discharged and one admitted.	
do.	4/2/17		Major Lake, the Senior Supply Officer, for O.C. Divisional Train, inspected the transport.	
do.	5/2/17		No. S.E. 9790, Pte J.H. Taylor, A.V.C. reported for duty from No. 114 Veterinary Hospital ABBEVILLE and was taken on the strength, this man replaced No. S.E. 6114 Pte. F. Hall, A.V.C., who was evacuated to Hospital.	
do.	6/2/17		The A.D.V.S. with the D.A.Q.M.G., visited the Section.	
do.	7/2/17		Two animals were admitted.	
do.	8/2/17		A movement order was received from A.D.V.S. giving instructions for the Section to move to BRAY on 11/2/17 and take over from the 15th M.V.S., 8th Division.	
do.	9/2/17		Two animals were admitted.	
do.	10/2/17		The A.D.V.S. inspected animals. Two animals were admitted and 1 animal destroyed.	
do.	11/2/17		The Section moved from CHIPILLY to BRAY after handing over billet to 15th M.V.S. Their billet in BRAY was taken over and also 26 animals for evacuation. 1 N.C.O. and 3 men were detached from the 15th M.V.S. for duty with us. A wire was received from the A.D.V.S. saying evacuations could proceed in moderation.	
BRAY	12/2/17		A.D.V.S. notified no evacuation could take place from BRAY to-morrow. Arrangements were made with R.T.O. for trucks.	
do.	13/2/17		Forty-six animals (16 from 110th Divn) were evacuated from BRAY.	

Army Form C. 2118

WAR DIARY
or
INTELLIGENCE SUMMARY
(Erase heading not required.)

Instructions regarding War Diaries and Intelligence Summaries are contained in F. S. Regs., Part II. and the Staff Manual respectively. Title Pages will be prepared in manuscript.

Place	Date	Hour	Summary of Events and Information	Remarks and references to Appendices
BRAY	14/2/17		Forty five animals were received and one destroyed.	
do.	15/2/17		The A.D.V.S. came to give new arrangements re evacuations. In future, these are to take place on Tuesdays and Saturdays; the maximum number from each Division is not to exceed 40 animals per week.	
BRAY	16/2/17		A wire was received from A.D.V.S. that evacuation is suspended until Tuesday 20/2/17	
do.	17/2/17		Two animals were admitted and one died	
do.	18/2/17		The A.D.V.S. wired that animals can be evacuated from PLATEAU and ALBERT only.	
do.	19/2/17		Animals for evacuation were inspected by the A.D.V.S. and arrangements were made to evacuate from PLATEAU (MARICOURT). Map reference ALBERT (combined sheet - A 20 c. 10.9.)	
do.	20/2/17		Forty four animals were evacuated from PLATEAU by special hospital train.	
do.	21/2/17		Capt. Lancaster gave a lecture to the farriers of the 40th Divnl. train on "The Diseases of the Horse's foot"	
do.	22/2/17		No. SE 4242 Corpl. E. Elliott was admitted to hospital sick. A wire was received from the A.D.V.S. saying evacuation could proceed on Saturday in usual way from nearest Railhead.	
do.	23/2/17		The A.D.V.S. inspected animals for evacuation. No. SE 4625 A/L. Corpl. Phillips was admitted to hospital sick.	
do.	24/2/17		Twenty one animals (including 5 skin cases) were evacuated from BRAY. Two animals were destroyed and their hides sent to the Base.	
do.	25/2/17		Two animals were admitted and one destroyed.	
do.	26/2/17		Four animals were admitted.	
do.	27/2/17		Two animals (cases of Ulcerative Cellulitis) were evacuated from BRAY and 3 hides were sent to the Base	
do.	28/2/17		One animal was destroyed. The O.C. visited 135th Field Ambulance to inspect animals as Stomatitis was reported in an animal after its evacuation from that unit.	

SHEET I
Army Form C. 2118

WAR DIARY
or
INTELLIGENCE SUMMARY
(Erase heading not required.)

Instructions regarding War Diaries and Intelligence Summaries are contained in F. S. Regs., Part II. and the Staff Manual respectively. Title Pages will be prepared in manuscript.

Place	Date	Hour	Summary of Events and Information	Remarks and references to Appendices
BRAY	1/3/17		Four animals were admitted.	
do.	2/3/17		Five animals were admitted.	
do.	3/3/17		Twenty-one sick animals were evacuated from BRAY. The A.D.V.S. inspected these prior to evacuation.	
do.	4/3/17		The O.C. visited SUZANNE to arrange to take over from 43rd M.V.S., 33rd Div'n. 51 Corpl. Phelps reported back for duty from 101st Field Ambulance.	
do.	5/3/17		Six animals were admitted.	
do.	6/3/17		Six animals were evacuated from BRAY and twenty-three hides received from 4th Reserve Park, A.S.C., were sent to the Base.	
do.	7/3/17		One animal was admitted.	
do.	9/3/17		The Section moved from BRAY to SUZANNE and took over billets vacated by the 43rd M.V.S., 33rd Division. Eight animals for evacuation were taken over from them.	
SUZANNE	10/3/17		Twenty-eight sick animals were evacuated from BRAY. The A.D.V.S. inspected these prior to entrainment.	
do.	11/3/17		Four animals were admitted.	
do.	12/3/17		The A.D.V.S. inspected animals for evacuation.	
do.	13/3/17		Eighteen animals were evacuated from BRAY.	
do.	14/3/17		Five animals were admitted. As the horses of the Lewis Machine Gun Officers were withdrawn from them these surplus animals were sent on to the Section for disposal.	
do.	15/3/17		The A.D.V.S. inspected the surplus chargers received. Nine were found unfit for issue and seven fit.	

1875 Wt. W593/826 1,000,000 4/15 I.B.C. & A. A.D.S.S./Forms/C.2118.

SHEET II
Army Form C. 2118

WAR DIARY
or
INTELLIGENCE SUMMARY
(Erase heading not required.)

Instructions regarding War Diaries and Intelligence Summaries are contained in F.S. Regs., Part II. and the Staff Manual respectively. Title Pages will be prepared in manuscript.

Place	Date	Hour	Summary of Events and Information	Remarks and references to Appendices
SUZANNE	16/3/17		A wire was received from the A.P.M. to send an escort to AMIENS to conduct back No. S.E. 8383 Pte. Rosser and No. S.E. A104 Pte. Roberts. Animals for evacuation were inspected by A.D.V.S.	
do.	17/3/17		Thirty two sick animals were evacuated from BRAY. An escort of 1 N.C.O. and two men left BRAY for AMIENS to report to A.P.M. of that town.	
do.	18/3/17		The escort reported back from AMIENS with the two prisoners. Animals for evacuation were inspected by the A.D.V.S.	
do.	19/3/17			
do.	20/3/17		Fifty four sick animals were evacuated from BRAY.	
do.	21/3/17		Orders were received from the A.D.V.S. for the Section to move to CURLU (Map reference Sheet 62c - A 29 central).	
			No. S.E. 8383 Pte. Rosser and No. S.E. A104 Pte. Roberts were tried for "When on Active Service – absent from unit until apprehended by M.F.P. in AMIENS" – 6 hours absence. Each was sentenced to 7 days No. 2 F.P.	
do.	22/3/17		The Section moved from SUZANNE to CURLU. Sixty three animals, some under treatment and the rest awaiting evacuation were taken.	
			No. S.E. 13970 Sergt. Montague with 2 drivers R.E.A and 4 horses reported and were taken on the ration strength. These animals were the remainder of the Stomatitis cases which had been treated at 11th Reserve Park A.S.C.	
do.	23/3/17		No. S.E. 1673 Pte. Playford was appointed acting corporal pending confirmation to rank of paid acting corporal in place of No. S.E. W242 P/A/Corpl Elliott evacuated.	

1875 Wt. W593/826 1,000,000 4/15 T.R.C. & A. A.D.S.S./Forms/C. 2118.

SHEET III
Army Form C. 2118

WAR DIARY
or
INTELLIGENCE SUMMARY
(Erase heading not required.)

Instructions regarding War Diaries and Intelligence Summaries are contained in F.S. Regs., Part II. and the Staff Manual respectively. Title Pages will be prepared in manuscript.

No. 51 Mobile Veterinary ... No. 10 ... 31/3/17

Place	Date	Hour	Summary of Events and Information	Remarks and references to Appendices
CURLU	24/3/17		Thirty-nine animals were evacuated from MARICOURT BOIS rail Head. These animals were inspected by the A.D.V.S. the preceding day.	
do.	25/3/17		Gunner Booth who was attached from B/175 Bde, R.F.A., reported back to his unit	
do.	26/3/17		Animals for evacuation were inspected by A.D.V.S.	
do.	27/3/17		Seven animals were evacuated from MARICOURT BOIS. Pte. Owen, of B Coy, 18th Welsh Regt. reports for duty from Divisional Headquarters and was taken on the ration strength.	
do.	28/3/17		The A.D.V.S. inspected animals for evacuation.	
do.	29/3/17		Confirmation of the appointment of No.S.E.1073 Pte Playford to L/P/Corporal was received from the D.D.V.S.	
do.	30/3/17		No.S.E.12992 Pte. Cornish reported for duty from No.3 Veterinary Hospital, BOULOGNE and was taken on the strength, thus completing the Section to War Establishment.	
do.	31/3/17		Twenty animals were evacuated from MARICOURT BOIS. These were inspected by the A.D.V.S. on the preceding day	

WAR DIARY
or
INTELLIGENCE SUMMARY.
(Erase heading not required.)

Army Form C. 2118.

Mob Vety Sec

Vol XI

Place	Date	Hour	Summary of Events and Information	Remarks and references to Appendices
MOISLAINS	23/4/17		The A.D.V.S. inspected animals for evacuation and a wire was received from both R.T.O. of QUINCONCE and FLAMICOURT Railheads, PÉRONNE saying sick animals could now be evacuated from there.	
do.	25/4/17		The A.D.V.S. visited the Section to make arrangements for the formation of a Rest Station for animals of the Division in need of a rest. A Divisional Routine Order was published giving particulars and a copy is given.*	*Appendix III
do.	28/4/17		A fatigue party of 20 men from the 20th Middlesex Regt reported for duty to help to prepare rest station for horses. Water troughs were supplied and a pump, also tents for the accommodation of men attached. A paddock on the other side of the stream (TORTILLE R.) has been secured. The horses are brushed over in the morning and turned out into the paddock where they remain till dusk. No watering or feeding takes place in the stables for besides watering troughs feeding troughs have been erected in the paddock. These are filled with chaff and oats and bran ad lib. Nets full of hay await the horses on their entry to stables at night."	
do.	30/4/17		The A.D.V.S. visited the Section and inspected the rest Camp. An order was received from A.D.V.S. that owing to reduction in establishment of M.V.S. 5 Riders were to be sent to H.QM D.A.C.	

Mob Vety Sec
(5 Riders
O.C. 5th M.V.S.)

Army Form C. 2118.

WAR DIARY
or
INTELLIGENCE SUMMARY.
(Erase heading not required.)

Instructions regarding War Diaries and Intelligence Summaries are contained in F.S. Regs., Part II. and the Staff Manual respectively. Title pages will be prepared in manuscript.

Place	Date	Hour	Summary of Events and Information	Remarks and references to Appendices
MOISLAINS	16/4/17		Animals for evacuation were inspected by the D.D.V.S.	
do	17/4/17		Twenty-nine animals were evacuated from MARICOURT Railhead. As reports have been received about animals falling down in the trucks and being destroyed on arrival at the Base, in future, the N.C.O. i/c of conducting party is to report, on return, the state of the animals during the journey and their condition, on arrival at the Base.	
do	20/4/17		The A.D.V.S. inspected animals for evacuation.	
do	21/4/17		Sixteen sick animals were evacuated from MARICOURT BOIS. No.S.E.13970 Sergt. J.H. Montague, A.V.C., who was attacked in charge of STOMATITIS cases, was, on instructions from A.D.V.S., despatched to No.2 Veterinary Hospital, HAVRE. Sergt. Finch reported back from England.	
do	23/4/17		Owing to the formation of Corps Mobile Veterinary Detachments, the following N.C.O. and men reported for duty to V.O. i/c XVth Corps Vet. Gp., at ST. DENIS, PÉRONNE. No.S.E.1073 Corpl. Playford, No.S.E.5940 Pte. Banfoot, No.S.E. 12992 Pte. Conrad and No.B.E.11984 Pte. Madden. Particulars of these Corps Mobile Veterinary Detachments were given in 4th Army Routine Order No. 814 of 11th April 1917.	

Army Form C. 2118.

WAR DIARY
or
INTELLIGENCE SUMMARY.
(Erase heading not required.)

Instructions regarding War Diaries and Intelligence Summaries are contained in F. S. Regs., Part II. and the Staff Manual respectively. Title pages will be prepared in manuscript.

Place	Date	Hour	Summary of Events and Information	Remarks and references to Appendices
CURLU	7/4/17	9am.	The Section marched from CURLU to MOISLAINS via CLERY-SUR-SOMME and HAUT-ALLAINES. Prior to leaving CURLU twenty seven sick animals were despatched to MARICOURT BOIS Railhead for evacuation.	
MOISLAINS	8/4/17	7am.	No. S.E. 9049 Serg't Finck, A.V.C. proceeded on leave to England (allotment was received from A.D.V.S. on preceding evening	
do.	9/4/17		Animals for evacuation were inspected by A.D.V.S. Owing to the severe weather and hard work, a good number of horses were received suffering from DEBILITY.	
do.	10/4/17	10am	Forty-seven sick animals were evacuated from MARICOURT BOIS. Owing to the distance (12 miles) to Railhead only animals which were judged able to go the distance and stand the journey were selected for evacuation.	
do.	13/4/17		The A.D.V.S. inspected animals for evacuation	
do.	14/4/17		Sixty-four sick animals were evacuated from MARICOURT BOIS. Enquiries were made if animals could be evacuated from PÉRONNE but no animals could be accepted for the present.	

WAR DIARY
or
INTELLIGENCE SUMMARY.
(Erase heading not required.)

Army Form C. 2118.

Place	Date	Hour	Summary of Events and Information	Remarks and references to Appendices
CURLU.			Animals received at the Section suffering from ULCERATIVE CELLULITIS have been treated for some time, with good results, by the injection of crude turpentine into the ulcers. A report on the method has been made and an extract from it is attached. (Appendix 2).	
do.	2/4/17		The A.D.V.S. visited the Section and inspected the animals for evacuation.	
do.	3/4/17		Twelve sick animals were evacuated to FORGES from MARICOURT BOIS.	
do.	4/4/17		As A.D.V.S. informed the O.C. that the Division was moving into the line and that the Section would be located at MOISLAINS. Capt Lancaster went to make arrangements for billets. A very suitable place was obtained, the remains of a factory. It had been damaged by shell fire but inside was a red brick floor, a good standing for horses, especially foot cases. An abundant water supply was near at hand. TORTILLE River, a tributary of the River SOMME flowed past near hand.	"X" Map Appendix I
do.	5/4/17		Orders were received from the A.D.V.S. for the Section to move to MOISLAINS on 7th/6th April.	
do.	6/4/17		Sergt Brown and 2 men proceeded to MOISLAINS as advance party to take over billets -	

APPENDIX I

SHEET 62c.

MOISLAINS
HAUT-ALLAINES
FEUILLAUCOURT
To PÉRONNE
To BOUCHAVESNES + RANCOURT
CLERY-SUR-SOMME
CURLU
To MAUREPAS
SOMME BASIN
TORTILLE R.

APPENDIX II

EXTRACT FROM REPORT BY CAPTAIN G.C. LANCASTER, A.V.C. ON THE TREATMENT OF ULCERATIVE CELLULITIS BY THE INJECTION OF TURPENTINE.

<u>Procedure.</u>   The ulcers were washed with warm water to which a little creosote had been added, then dried, and afterwards injected with turpentine.

My first method was to inject the ulcers with a Hypodermic Syringe, each ulcer receiving ½ c.c., after which it was bandaged, and similarly injected and bandaged on alternate days.

I was extremely careful that the syringe was pushed into the ulcer as far as it was thought the cavity went, which in bad ulcers was often an inch or an inch and a half.

That method was found to be very effective, for the ulcers showed signs of healing after two or three injections, but during 10 days I broke three needles and used a considerable amount of bandages and wool, consequently a less extravagant method was devised, which was equally effective, and did away with the Hypodermic Syringe and needles, and also the bandages, and which was the following :-

All legs were left unbandaged, no matter how bad they were, and after being washed with warm water and a little creosote, were injected daily with the large brass syringe (4 oz) and a metal nozzle. A strong solution of disinfectant in warm water was kept in a bucket, and the nozzle was washed in this after each injection, with the view of not spreading the disease to new areas.

By this syringe there are no means of measuring

APPENDIX II (2)

measuring the amount of turpentine injected, but as that appears to be of no moment and it saved the breakage of needles, such a method was afterwards adhered to. The syringe full would do about 8 or 10 animals, some of which had 20 ulcers on their legs, and in consequence, took about an ounce of turpentine, but after three or four injections it was often a difficulty to get the nozzle in at all, so only new ulcers required looking for.

The large metal nozzle was inserted into the ulcers as far as it would easily go, and turpentine was injected until the cavity of the ulcers was full, and afterwards, turpentine and whale oil, 1–4 was smeared over them.

In one particular case of a newly formed ulcer I treated amongst my first batch with the Hypodermic needle and a bandage, all the dead tissue (core) sloughed out on the 2nd day when the first bandage was taken off.

There were no signs of constitutional disturbance — not one of the patients ever required any medicine except when first admitted, serious cases were given a dose of physic.

For a local treatment and until a specific vaccine is obtained, the Turpentine Injections are, in my opinion, remarkably good and well worth a trial — just the injection into the ulcers of crude turpentine and no bandages used whatever.

(3)

During the short time that I used it I treated 25 cases, 10 of which were discharged and 3 I have still with me - one ready to discharge and two others nearly cured - the others I have had most reluctantly to evacuate to the Base the other day because of our constant moving about and uncertainty of obtaining any standings it was impossible for me to treat them any longer. However 11 out of the 12 were doing well, but one had formed a nasty ulcer right up in the thigh along the lymphatics which had developed during the march, but all these low down on the leg had nearly all healed up.

Also amongst those 12 evacuated were cases where previous to being sent to me had had the ulcers fired with some sort of a budding iron and in consequence had left large granulations with permanently thickened legs. These did not respond to the treatment as well as the others but will, I think, come right in time, for the ulcers were healing quite satisfactorily but there were the large granulations caused by the hot iron to contend with.

After the injections, the animals with the deep ulcers, which required a fair amount of turpentine showed signs of irritation immediately afterwards. They stamped and somewhat tried to lick their legs

legs, but the pain very soon passed (4) away. I may add that I had attended using a mixed vaccine along with the turpentine injection but the vaccine was unobtainable from Veterinary Stores and in consequence I have had no chance of combining the two treatments, but should very much like to try at the first opportunity although I am every day anticipating the information that a specific vaccine for ULCERATIVE CELLULITIS has been found.

A Short Summary of 6 cases.

1/ Grey H.D. mare A.S.C. Horse, badly infected on its near hind. The animal was treated with boric & lime. Copper sulphate ointment and oily dressing and various dry dressings and its leg got worse, eventually developing nearly a score of ulcers. After a month's treatment it is now nearly ready for discharge to the unit. This was a remarkably bad & stubborn case.

2/ Rider near hind leg infected with 2 large ulcers, discharged cured after 4 injections in 18 days.

3/ Black H.D. mare O.H. infected, had been under treatment two weeks before being sent to me as it was an animal the unit particularly wanted to keep. Several small ulcers on the pastern, admitted 26th Feb. - discharged cured 19/3/17.

(5)

4/ Bay Gelding. Ulcers on O.H. and nose. The nose ulcer was cured after 3 injections and this animal was returned to its unit after two weeks treatment but the ulcer on the leg had not properly healed up but sufficient to allow it to return to duty and especially as that battalion was moving and they were being very short of horses.

5/ Brown Gelding, L.D., from Artillery – 2 ulcers on its near hind, discharged cured in 13 days.

6/ Bay Gelding L.D. from Artillery – ulcers on its off hind, discharged cured in 14 days.

From my little experience I find that from 2 to 5 weeks is sufficient to treat the ordinary cases of ULCERATIVE CELLULITIS. which are being sent to M.V.Ss. for evacuation and as soon as circumstances permit I shall very much like to treat some more. A careful watch is being kept to see if any of these cases are returned but so far none have as yet come. It is now 3 weeks since I discharged some of the earlier cases. If dry standings such as are in hospitals can be obtained the above treatment is well worth a trial as you will see from the above report.

(Sd) G.C. Lancaster, Capt. AVC
O.C. 5¹ᵗ M.V.S

P.S / MODIFIED TREATMENT
After cavity of ulcer has filled up superficial scar is treated with crystals of Pot. Perman.

APPENDIX III

ROUTINE ORDERS
-by-
Major General H.G. RUGGLES-BRISE, C.B., M.V.O.,
COMMANDING 40th DIVISION.

1100. 1100.

REST STATION FOR ANIMALS.

A 40th Division rest station is being formed for animals requiring rest, veterinary attendance and special feeding. It will be attached to 51st Mobile Veterinary Section situated at MOISLAINS, and will be open on the 28th April, 1917.

Animals requiring rest and treatment will be selected by Veterinary Officers of units concerned.

One man is to be sent with every four animals, or fraction of four; it is essential that only reliable men are sent.

A nose bag, head collar and rope, a rug, grooming kit and a full day's rations are to be sent with each animal.

They will be frequently inspected by the A.D.V.S, who will decide when they are fit to return to their units.

Officers are required to visit their animals while in the rest station and take an active interest in them.

Should the Division move, the animals and the men looking after them will be at once returned to their respective units.

By making use of the rest station it is anticipated that evacuations will be reduced and animals will be saved for units, which otherwise would eventually become debility cases & sent to the Base

WAR DIARY or INTELLIGENCE SUMMARY.

Army Form C. 2118.

51 Mob. Vety. Sec

8 of 12

Place	Date	Hour	Summary of Events and Information	Remarks and references to Appendices
MOISLAINS Map Reference: Sheet 62C C.12c.7,5.	1/5/17		The A.D.V.S. and D.A.Q.M.G. inspected the horse Rest Camp. Several transport officers visited to see their animals.	
	2/5/17		Notification was received from the A.D.V.S. that the Establishment of horses of the Section was reduced by five riders and that the five riders were to be given to the French Mission for the use of the interpreters attached to Brigades and Divisional Headquarters.	
do.	3/5/17		These five surplus riders were issued to the Liaison Officer. Divnl. Hd. Qrs., also four saddles and bridles. The remaining saddles and bridles was returned to the Ordnance Stores.	
do.	4/5/17		An operation was performed on a grey mare, admitted with a gunshot wound on the near buttock, said to be caused by an explosion of ammunition being carried in a wagon. She nose cap of an English 18 pounder shell was extracted from the rear side of the animal. It was hoped the mare would live but it had to be destroyed two days after. Enquiries were made into the cause of the explosion and the result of these is given in Appendix I. Animals for evacuation were inspected by the A.D.V.S.	
do.	7/5/17		Twenty-out animals were evacuated from Quinconce Railhead, PÉRONNE to No.7 Veterinary Hospital, FORGES-LES-EAUX.	
do.	8/5/17			
do.	9/5/17		A light draught mare admitted 3 days ago with a gunshot wound on	

Sheet II

Army Form C. 2118.

WAR DIARY
or
INTELLIGENCE SUMMARY.
(Erase heading not required.)

Place	Date	Hour	Summary of Events and Information	Remarks and references to Appendices
			The off shore was destroyed. A post mortem was held and a bullet was found embedded in the bone and the distal end of the radius fractured.	
MOISLAINS	10/5/17		In accordance with instructions received from the A.D.V.S., the O.C. attended a lecture at the Divisional Gas School, FINS, on "Horse Respirators"	
do.	11/5/17		The A.D.V.S. inspected animals for evacuation and horses in Rest Camp ready for discharge. No. S.E. 11952 Sergt Brown, A.V.C. attended a lecture at FINS on "Horse Respirators"	
do.	12/5/17		Twenty five animals were evacuated from QUINCONCE Railhead PERONNE. to enable the horses being watered en route petrol tins, free of water are placed in the trucks. These are taken over at the Base and results given for them.	
do.	13/5/17		The A.D.V.S. of the Fourth Army, Colonel Hunt, accompanied by the A.D.V.S., Major Rorston, inspected the Section, the sick animals under treatment and horses in the Rest Camp.	
do.	15/5/17		Twenty animals were evacuated to the Base from the same Railhead. Horse hides and empty tracking cases were also sent to No. 7 Veterinary Hospital —	

Army Form C. 2118.

WAR DIARY
or
INTELLIGENCE SUMMARY.
(Erase heading not required.)

Instructions regarding War Diaries and Intelligence Summaries are contained in F. S. Regs. Part II. and the Staff Manual respectively. Title pages will be prepared in manuscript.

Place	Date	Hour	Summary of Events and Information	Remarks and references to Appendices
MOISLAINS	19/5/17		Nineteen animals were evacuated to the Base. Thirteen were rejected by the A.D.V.S. the remaining eight to experience at the Railhead the want of the animals no certified items in the actual time.	
"	21/5/17		The animals for evacuation were seen by the A.D.V.S. who at first rejected 3 animals which were suffering from sores in uses (ambulance cases) were returned as being unfit to travel.	
"	22/5/17		Eight animals were despatched to the Base from PERONNE. Instructions are verbal ones to the N.C.O. i/c of entraining party to report any case of rough shunting to the R.T.O. at the first station stating what also written instructions are given when the men are not to leave a gate in one truck that lead one to travel all the journey in the truck allotted to him.	
"	26/5/17		Five animals were returned to unit from the Rest Camp.	
"	28/5/17		The A.D.V.S. saw the animals for evacuation.	
"	29/5/17		Fifteen animals were sent to the Base. Among them was one with Strand-Halis. We want to keep from stables for a further trial. This animal was evacuated as a Roarer.	
"	30/5/17 31/5/17		Routine work.	

END.

APPENDIX I

With reference to your request for an account of the accident which resulted in a riding wheeler of No. 2 Section being severely wounded, I have gone into the matter and the following are the circumstances.

A convoy of six wagons of ammunition were being taken up to a battery position. They arrived at a point about 300 yards off the guns when it was noticed that one of the wagon bodies was on fire. The N.C.O. i/c and the drivers all agree that no noise was heard and they think the fire originated in the wagon body.

Personally I think there is no doubt that the wagon was hit by a 77mm shell and owing to the noise made by the wheels, the drivers did not hear anything. The Germans were certainly shelling at the time and the wagon is marked on the outside as by a shell.

The wagon was packed with high explosive shells, the fuses of which are not at all sensitive, and I think the cordite charges must have been set on fire by a hostile shell, which in turn set fire to the wicker work fittings of the body and set the fuse off, and detonated the shell.

Beyond a shaking, none of the drivers were in any way hurt although the force of the explosion was sufficient to blow off both the centre and wheel drivers steel helmets.

(Sd) A.G. Brown, Lt. & Adjt.
40th D.A.C.

Army Form C. 2118.

WAR DIARY
or
INTELLIGENCE SUMMARY.
(Erase heading not required.)

Place	Date	Hour	Summary of Events and Information	Remarks and references to Appendices
MOISLAINS (Sheet 62 - C.12)	1/6/17		Animals for evacuation were inspected by the A.D.V.S. Animals in the Rest Camp were also examined. A 2½% solution of formalin was tried for Ulcerative Cellulitis but was not a success. After injection a very hard black scar formed on the surface which was impossible to wash off and in consequence the lower portion of the ulcer could not be accessed.	
do.	2/6/17		Nine animals were evacuated to No.1 Veterinary Hospital FORGES-LES-EAUX from PÉRONNE and ten animals were discharged to their units from the Rest Camp.	
do.	3/6/17		No.S.E. 11952 Sergt. J. Brown, A.V.C. proceeded to England on leave. In accordance with instructions received a horse was collected from SUZANNE. It had been left in charge of an inhabitant there by the 2nd Batt. Kings Regt., 8th Division.	
do.	4/6/17		Instructions in the use of "Anti-gas Horse Respirators" were received from the A.D.V.S., also one of the Respirators for demonstration purposes. A.V.C. sergeants are to understand their use and put one on a horse in presence of a veterinary officer. Instructions were also received from the A.D.V.S. that a B.C. Horse has been discovered for the treatment of Ulcerative Cellulitis in its very early stages and that cases were to be evacuated promptly.	

WAR DIARY
or
INTELLIGENCE SUMMARY.
(Erase heading not required.)

Army Form C. 2118.

Place	Date	Hour	Summary of Events and Information	Remarks and references to Appendices
MOISLAINS	5/6/17	2 pm	Impalpable Iodoform Powder is to be tried in the treatment of Ophthalmia and a report submitted in due course as to its efficacy. Capt. Lancaster A.V.C. O.C. the Section gave a lecture to the men on the use of "Anti-gas Horse Respirators" One was fitted on a horse and the animal trotted whilst wearing it.	
do	6/6/17		Every case of "picked up nail" is to be reported now in writing by V.O.s to the Headquarters of units to which the animal belongs in order that enquiries can be made to see if the preventative measures laid down are being carried out. These measures include the placing of boxes marked "NAILS" at dumps and places where nails are likely to be found; the withdrawal of nails from all boxes prior to burning (especially in Field Kitchens); units to be responsible for the picking up of nails in and around their billets.	
do	8/6/17		No. 7.065334 Driver Stonnell, D.S.C. attached to the Section proceeded to England on leave. The A.D.V.S. inspected animals for evacuation. Thirty animals were evacuated, including thirteen from Corps Troops.	
do	9/6/17		Routine Work.	
do	11/6/17 Monday			
do	12/6/17		Five cases of Ulcerative Cellulitis were evacuated. These had been inspected by the A.D.V.S. the previous evening.	
do	13/6/17		Routine Work.	

Army Form C. 2118.

WAR DIARY
or
INTELLIGENCE SUMMARY.
(Erase heading not required.)

Place	Date	Hour	Summary of Events and Information	Remarks and references to Appendices
MOISLAINS	14/6/17		The clipping of animals (especially mules) in the Rest Camp, although in summer, was found advantageous. It was found the animals thrived well and put on condition quicker.	
do	15/6/17		Animals for evacuation and all the animals in the Rest Camp were inspected by the A.D.V.S. Twenty seven of the latter were selected for discharge.	
do	16/6/17		Thirteen animals were evacuated, including two a horse and a mule cast by the D.D.R. 4th Army as "old and worn out" and recommended to be cast and sold for work on the land. No. S.E. 11952 Sergt J. Brown reported back from leave.	
do	17/6/17		Twenty seven animals were discharged to their units from the Rest Camp.	
do	19/6/17		Eight animals were evacuated. There had been seen the previous day by the D.V.S.	
do	20/6/17		No. S.E. 1934 Corpl Evans left for England on leave.	
do	21/6/17		No. T.065334 Driver Bromwell A.S.C. reported back from leave.	
do	23/6/17		Seven animals were evacuated after inspection the by the A.D.V.S. the day previously.	
do	24/6/17		Lt. Col. The Gerrard, A.V.C., the A.D.V.S, 3rd Corps waited and inspected the Section.	
do	25/6/17		Capt. Leinbach A.V.C., OC the Section took over the duties of Acting D.A.D.V.S., during the absence on leave, of Major W.N. Rowston, D.A.D.V.S, of the Division.	
do	26/6/17		A wire was received from ADVS, that a H.D. horse of No.1 Coy, 40th Divnl Train, A.S.C. had reached and ordered all animals in the Section and also in the 40th Divnl Train.	

Army Form C. 2118.

WAR DIARY
or
INTELLIGENCE SUMMARY.
(Erase heading not required.)

Instructions regarding War Diaries and Intelligence Summaries are contained in F.S. Regs., Part II. and the Staff Manual respectively. Title pages will be prepared in manuscript.

Place	Date	Hour	Summary of Events and Information	Remarks and references to Appendices
MOISLAINS	27/6/17	8.15am	All animals in Section, 52 horses and 4 mules in all, were tested for Glanders by the Intra-dermo palpebral Mallein Test.	
do.	28/6/17		No reactor was found among the animals malleined	
do.	29/6/17		Lt.Col.the.Gowan A.D.V.S, 3rd Corps and Lt.Col.Lort Phillips, 3rd Corps advisor in horsemanship visited the Section.	
do.	30/6/17		Thirteen animals were evacuated from PERONNE	
			APPENDIX.	
			Number of animals dealt with by the Section during the month.	
			Animals remaining on May 31st ... 74	
			Animals admitted in June ... 106	
			TOTAL 180	
			DISPOSAL. Evacuated ... 85	
			Died ... Nil.	
			Destroyed ... 3	
			Missing ... Nil.	
			Discharged to Units from Rest tank 48	
			Discharged to Units Cured 10	
			Cured and raised as Remounts 6	
			Surplus (found) raised as Remounts 2	
			Remaining on June 30th 26	
			TOTAL 180	

Army Form C. 2118.

WAR DIARY
or
INTELLIGENCE SUMMARY.
(Erase heading not required.)

Instructions regarding War Diaries and Intelligence Summaries are contained in F.S. Regs., Part II. and the Staff Manual respectively. Title pages will be prepared in manuscript.

Place	Date	Hour	Summary of Events and Information	Remarks and references to Appendices
MOISLAINS.	1/7/17		Arrangements were made with O.C. IIIrd Corps Mobile Veterinary Detachment to replace three men attached there by three others.	
do.	2/7/17		No.8381 Pte. Borrens, No.8383 Pte. Rossio and No.17167 Pte. Woodstock reported for duty to IIIrd Corps Mob. Vet. Detachment to replace Ptes. Madden, Cornick and Banfort.	
do.	3/7/17		No. S.E. 9333 a/Corpl. McLoughlin proceeded to England on leave. A new horse ambulance arrived at the Section. This was to replace an unserviceable one. The old one was a French pattern and much lighter than the new one. The old float was found very useful in winter time for gaining access to muddy horse lines in the SOMME valley.	
do.	4/7/17		Corpl. Evans reported back from leave from England. Corpl. Evans was sent to IIInd Corps M.V.D. to replace Corpl. Playford who returned to the Section.	
do.	5/7/17		a/Corpl. S.S. Oliver proceeded to England on leave.	
do.	6th 7th		Routine Work.	
do.	8th		One animal was discharged from the Rest Camp.	
do.	9/7/17		A return of A.V.C. personnel with the Section is to be sent weekly to the D.A.D.V.S., to reach his office by Friday evening.	

WAR DIARY or INTELLIGENCE SUMMARY

Army Form C. 2118.

July 1917

Place	Date	Hour	Summary of Events and Information	Remarks and references to Appendices
MOISLAINS	10/7/17		Twenty-one animals were evacuated to No. 7 Vety Hospital from PÉRONNE.	
do.	11/7/17		A memo. was received from D.A.D.V.S. saying all water troughs in Divisional Area are to be thoroughly scrubbed inside and outside once a week with a solution of chloride of lime 1 part and water 1000 parts. A Divisional Order makes units in their area responsible for this.	
do.	12/7/13		Routine Work.	
do.	14/7/17		Circular memo. No. 25 was received from D.A.D.V.S. saying the D.D.R. 3rd Army was willing to abide by the verdict of A.D. do V.S. am Corps and D.A.D. do V.S. Divisions re the re-classification of animals provided he were informed through the "Q" branch of formations concerned.	
do.	15/7/17		An advanced collecting station from the Section was opened at NURLU (Sht 62c – U 28 d 8.6.) Sergt Finch being placed in charge.	
do.	16/7/17		No. 222 Staff Sergt Westwood reported from No. 7 Vety. Hospital for duty with the Section and was taken on the strength.	
do.	17/7/17		A/Corpl McLoughlin reported back from leave and No. 4628 L/Corpl Pheebs proceeded to England on leave.	
do.	18/7/17		The remaining animals in the Rest Camp were inspected by the D.A.D.V.S.	

Army Form C. 2118.

WAR DIARY
or
INTELLIGENCE SUMMARY.
(Erase heading not required.)

Instructions regarding War Diaries and Intelligence Summaries are contained in F.S. Regs., Part II. and the Staff Manual respectively. Title pages will be prepared in manuscript.

Place	Date	Hour	Summary of Events and Information	Remarks and references to Appendices
HORSLAINES	19/7/17		a/Cpl S.S. Oliver returned back from leave.	
do	20/7/17		The animals for evacuation were inspected by the D.A.D.V.S.	
do	21/7/17		Fifteen animals were evacuated to No.7 Vet: Hospital from PERONNE.	
do	22/7/17		Memo. was received from D.A.D.V.S. saying the number of cases of mange and suspected mange remaining under treatment in the Section is to be shown on the back of A.F. A2000 (Return of Sick and Injured Animals) Routine Work.	
do	24/7/17		Major Gordon (the D.A.Q.M.G.) visited the Section and advised the construction of winter shelters for horses. Routine Work.	
do	25/7/17		Animals for evacuation were inspected by the D.A.D.V.S.	
do	26/7/17			
do	27/7/17		Twenty animals were evacuated.	
do	28/7/17		The erection of winter quarters is being proceeded with, the horse standings are good and nose shelters are being erected. Damaged huts are being returned for the accommodation of the men.	
do	29/7/17			
do	30/7/17		L/Cpl P. Phillips returned back from leave.	
do	31/7/17			

APPENDIX — OVER

WAR DIARY
or
INTELLIGENCE SUMMARY.

(Erase heading not required.)

Army Form C. 2118.

July 1917.

APPENDIX

The number of animals dealt with by the Section during the month of July 1917.

Number remaining on June 30th	26
Admitted in July	105
Total	131

DISPOSAL

Number evacuated	72
died	Nil
destroyed	1
missing	Nil
discharged	7
(a) from Rest Camp	
(b) to units cured	12
(c) Surplus as remounts	1
(d) to units – not with cases	2
Remaining on July 31st	36
Total	131

Army Form C. 2118.

WAR DIARY
or
INTELLIGENCE SUMMARY.
(Erase heading not required.)

S-1 Mot Vet Sec
Vol 15

Instructions regarding War Diaries and Intelligence Summaries are contained in F.S. Regs., Part II. and the Staff Manual respectively. Title pages will be prepared in manuscript.

Place	Date	Hour	Summary of Events and Information	Remarks and references to Appendices
MOISLAINS	1/8/17		Routine work.	
"	2/8/17		Routine work.	
"	3/8/17		ADVS inspected animals for evacuation	
"	4/8/17		13 animals evacuated to 7 Veterinary Hospital	
"	5/8/17		Routine work.	
"	6/8/17		Routine work.	
"	7/8/17		ADVS inspected animals in the Section	
"	8/8/17		Routine work.	
"	9/8/17		Routine work	
"	10/8/17		ADVS inspected animals for Evacuation	
"	11/8/17		Evacuated 8 animals to 7 Veterinary Hospital.	
"	12/8/17		Medical inspection of men of Section (exclusive of paid acting NCOs) Category 'A' men made out for transfer to Combatant Arms of the Service. List sent to ADVS Records.	
"	13/8/17		Routine work.	
"	14/8/17		ADVS inspected animals for evacuation under treatment. 5 animals suspected mange cases were evacuated to 7 Veterinary Hospital	
"	15/8/17		Routine work	
"	16/8/17		Routine work	
"	17/8/17		Routine work.	
"	18/8/17		13 animals Evacuated to Base No 7 Veterinary Hospital.	
"	19/8/17		Routine Work.	

WAR DIARY or INTELLIGENCE SUMMARY

Army Form C. 2118.

Place	Date	Hour	Summary of Events and Information	Remarks and references to Appendices
MOISLAINS	20/8/17		H⁰ Divisional Committee for selection of Broodmares viz. Major W.N. ROWSTON. DADVS. and Capt. J.R. RENWICK. DADVS. visited section, inspected all mares, rejected 4 Class I & 3 Class II Broodmares for final selection by III Corps Committee.	RF/3.
"	21/8/17		Routine work.	
"	22/8/17		No SE 20707. S/Smith PERKINS. E. reported from No 24 Veterinary Hospital for duty with Section	
"	23/8/17		Final inspection of Broodmares by III Corps Committee. 3 first class mares were selected.	
"	24/8/17		Capt G.C. LANCASTER proceeded to ENGLAND on 11 days leave. Capt P. HAUGH. A.V.C. took over the Section during his absence.	
"	25/8/17		No SE 102.05 P/A/Corpl. OLIVER. J.W. was transferred from 51st M.V.S. to No 24 Veterinary Hospital on being promoted to rank of Paid a/Corpl. Shoeing Smith. 18 animals were evacuated to No 9 Veterinary Hospital.	
"	26/8/17		Routine work	
"	27/8/17		A.D.V.S. III Corps inspected Section	
"	28/8/17		Routine work	
"	29/8/17		Routine work	
"	30/8/17		A.D.V.S. Third Army, accompanied by A.D.V.S. III Corps & DADVS 40 Division visited and inspected section.	
"	31/8/17		Routine work	

Peter Haugh Capt AVC
COMMANDING 51st MOBILE VET. SECTION

Army Form C. 2118.

WAR DIARY
or
INTELLIGENCE SUMMARY.
(Erase heading not required.)

51st Mobile Vet Section

9/1 16

Instructions regarding War Diaries and Intelligence Summaries are contained in F. S. Regs., Part II. and the Staff Manual respectively. Title pages will be prepared in manuscript.

Place	Date	Hour	Summary of Events and Information	Remarks and references to Appendices
MOISLAINS	1/9/17		Routine work	
	2/9/17		Order received from Lt Col McGowan. A.V.C. ADVS.III"Corps" Wounds are not to be washed before they are dressed. If there is any discharge, it should be removed with a piece of antiseptic cotton wool. The wound dressed & the surrounding parts cleaned with the wound dressing (Evsol for preference) The hair should be clipped away for several inches around all wounds on the skin. Any matted hair on which the discharge runs down should also be clipped away.	
"	3/9/17.		One Case of Suspected Glanders admitted. This animal was isolated in a covered in enclosure the place rubbed and of bounds. The driver of animal was sent to Section & attends to its grooming feeding. Animal is to be killed and Eye Mech on the 15th inst.	
"	4/9/17.		Routine work.	
"	5/9/17		No. 59440 S/Smith G. Barefoot & No 42672 S/Smith R Thompson proceeded to England on 11 days leave via LE HAVRE.	
"	6/9/17		Routine work.	
"	7/9/17		No. 222 S/Serg Westwood. S. & No 46496 Corpl. J. Betton. RFA attached 51M V.S. proceeded to England on 11 days leave via LE HAVRE. Capt J G Ramsactin AVC. returned from leave.	
"	8/9/17.		Evacuated 12 sick animals from QUINCONCE to No 1 Veterinary Hospital. FORGES-LES-EAUX. No 59244 Pte A. MILBURNE. was transferred to No 14104 Pte. E. W Roberts returned from leave. No 2 Section 40"D A.C. R.F.A	

Army Form C. 2118.

WAR DIARY
or
INTELLIGENCE SUMMARY.
(Erase heading not required.)

Instructions regarding War Diaries and Intelligence Summaries are contained in F. S. Regs., Part II. and the Staff Manual respectively. Title pages will be prepared in manuscript.

Place	Date	Hour	Summary of Events and Information	Remarks and references to Appendices
MOISLAINS	9/9/17		9 suspected Mange Cases with their Stable Headcollars & headropes were sent to III Corps Mange Bath at BEAUMETZ and were dipped.	
	10/9/17		Routine work.	
	11/9/17		—— do ——	
	12/9/17		—— do ——	
	13/9/17		—— do ——	
	14/9/17		9 ADVS inspected Section and animals for evacuation. Received wire from R.T.O. QUINCONCE that No sick animals could be evacuated from that railhead in future. Wired to FINS railhead & was informed that sick animals could be railed there on Tuesdays & Saturdays at 8.30 A.M.	
	15/9/17		One reinforcement reported from No 2 Veterinary Hospital. Nº SE 28432 Pte. S.C. LEE. Suspected Glanders Case was malleined in ?eck & ?ye.	
	16/9/17		Routine work.	
	17/9/17		9 Suspected Mange Cases were sent to III Corps Mange Bath at BEAUMETZ & dipped. DADVS 140 Division inspected animals for Evacuation.	
	18/9/17		Evacuated 14 sick animals from FINS to Nº 7 Veterinary Hospital FORGES-LES-EAUX.	

Army Form C. 2118.

WAR DIARY
or
INTELLIGENCE SUMMARY.
(Erase heading not required.)

Instructions regarding War Diaries and Intelligence Summaries are contained in F. S. Regs., Part II. and the Staff Manual respectively. Title pages will be prepared in manuscript.

Place	Date	Hour	Summary of Events and Information	Remarks and references to Appendices
MOISLAINS	19/9/17		No. SE 5940. Pt Basfort. C. returned from leave.	
"	20/9/17		Routine work.	
"	21/9/17		No. 222 S/Serg S. Eastwood & No. 46496. Corpls/Smith Beattson & RFA attached returned from leave.	
"	22/9/17		A.D.V.S. III Corps & D.A.D.V.S. 40" Division inspected Section.	
"	23/9/17		Routine work.	
"	24/9/17		D.A.D.V.S. 40" Div. inspected animals for evacuation.	
"	25/9/17		Evacuated 12 sick animals from FINS to No. 1 Veterinary Hospital FORGES-LES-EAUX.	
"	26/9/17		Routine work. No. 4762 S/Smith R. Thompson R.F.A attached, returned from leave.	
"	27/9/17		15 H.D. remounts & 9 men were billeted for the night on their way to units of 40" Division.	
"	28/9/17		D.A.D.V.S. 40" Division Inspected animals for Evacuation.	
"	29/9/17		A.D.V.S. III Army & A.D.V.S. III Corps Inspected Section. D.D.V.S. ordered Suspected Glanders case to be destroyed & a post mortem examination made. This was done and animal was found to have tumours on the Spectum nasi. 8 Sick animals were evacuated from FINS to No. 1 Veterinary Hospital FORGES-LES-EAUX.	
"	30/9/17		Routine work.	

WAR DIARY

INTELLIGENCE SUMMARY.
(Erase heading not required.)

OCTOBER 1917. Army Form C. 2118.

Mob Vety Sec

Vol 17

Place	Date	Hour	Summary of Events and Information	Remarks and references to Appendices
MOISLAINS	1/10/17		Animals for evacuation were inspected by the D.A.D.V.S.	
do.	2/10/17.		Eighteen animals were evacuated to No. 7 Vety. Hospital, FORGES-LES-EAUX.	
do.	3/10/17.		No. 20721 S. Smith Perkins was evacuated to No. 5 Casualty Clearing Station and was struck off the strength of the unit.	
do.	4/10/17.		Routine Work.	
do.	5/10/17.		The D.A.D.V.S. saw animals for evacuation.	
do.	6/10/17.		Eight animals were evacuated from FINS to FORGES. Pte Bowens and L. Corpl Phillips were admitted to III rd Corps Rest Station. The 32nd M.V.S. 20th Division, who are taking over from this Section marched into MOISLAINS and occupied billets adjacent to ours until billet was vacated by us.	
do	7/10/17		Routine Work.	
do.	8/10/17		The N.C.O. and 2 men were recalled from Advanced Collecting Station which was taken over by the 32nd M.V.S.	
do.	9/10/17		The N.C.O. and 3 men of the Section attached to III rd Corps Mobile Vety. Detachment were recalled.	
do.	10/10/17		Eight sick animals were handed over to 32nd M.V.S. It was not possible to evacuate them owing to the Section being under marching orders the following day.	
do.	11/10/17	8:30 a.m.	The Section proceeded by road to BAPAUME, and remained there the night.	
BAPAUME	12/10/17	9 a.m.	The Section marched to MONCHIET (PAS-DE-CALAIS). Covered standings	

WAR DIARY
OCTOBER 1917.   Army Form C. 2118.

or

INTELLIGENCE SUMMARY.

(Erase heading not required.)

Instructions regarding War Diaries and Intelligence Summaries are contained in F. S. Regs., Part II. and the Staff Manual respectively. Title pages will be prepared in manuscript.

Place	Date	Hour	Summary of Events and Information	Remarks and references to Appendices
			were available for the horses and huts for the mens' billet. There was a good water supply.	
MONCHIET	13/10/17		Pte Owen, 18th Welsh Regt, attached to the Section, proceeded to England on leave.	
do.	14+15/10/17		Routine Work	
do.	16/10/17		No. S.E. 11680 Pte. Allen, B., reported for duty from No. 4 Vety. Hospital and was taken on the strength.	
do.	17/10/17		A wire was received saying 7 reinforcements had left No. 6 Vety. Hospital, ROUEN. There are to replace 7 category "B" men.	
do.	18,19,20/10/17		Routine Work.	
do.	21/10/17		Seven category "B" men reported for duty	
do.	22/10/17		Seven "A" men from the Section proceeded to No.2 Vety. Hospital. The D.A.D.V.S. and O.C. Section expressed their appreciation of the good services rendered by these men whilst with the Section.	
do.	23/10/17		Routine Work	
do.	24/10/17		Six animals were evacuated from BEAUMETZ-RIVIÈRE to No.7 Vety. Hospital, FORGES.	
do.	25/10/17		Routine Work	
do.	26/10/17		Pte. Owen reported back from leave.	
do.	27/10/17		The D.A.D.V.S. saw sick animals. Owing to early moves 3 were evacuated and those under treatment were returned to their units.	
do.	28/10/17		Movement Order was received from D.A.D.V.S. The Section is to	

Army Form C. 2118.

WAR DIARY
or
INTELLIGENCE SUMMARY.

(Erase heading not required.)

OCTOBER 1917

Place	Date	Hour	Summary of Events and Information	Remarks and references to Appendices
MONCHIET	29/10/17		Proceed on 29th inst to WARLINCOURT-LES-PAS. Six animals were evacuated from BEAUMETZ-RIVIÈRE to FORGES.	
do.	do.	10am	The Section proceeded by road to WARLINCOURT-LES-PAS. No. S.E. 15019 Pte Carter proceeded to England on leave.	
WARLINCOURT LES-PAS	30/10/17		The D.A.D.V.S. visited the Section.	
do.	31/10/17		Routine Work.	

November 1917

51st M.V.S.

WAR DIARY
or
INTELLIGENCE SUMMARY.

Army Form C. 2118.

Place	Date	Hour	Summary of Events and Information	Remarks and references to Appendices
WARLINGCOURT -LEZ-PAS	1/11/17		1 mange case was admitted from 25th Field Coy. Canadian Forestry Corps.	
do.	2/11/17		Capt. Mc Indoo, Ptes. Maiden, Woodstock and Drivers Wharfe, Ashdown and Gain proceeded to England on 14 days' leave.	
do.	3/11/17		1 mange case was evacuated from BEAUMETZ-RIVIERE. No. 2547/17 Pte. J.B. Barrett, A.V.C. reported for duty from No. 24 Vety. Hospital and was taken on the strength.	
do.	5/11/17		No. 8383 Pte. Rossie reported back from leave to England. The D.A.D.V.S. visited and inspected the Section. Pte. Rossie was admitted to 135th Field Ambulance.	
do.	6/11/17		Pte. Rossie was evacuated from 125th Field Ambulance to the 3rd Canadian Stationary Hospital.	
do.	7/11/17		Routine Work.	
do.	8/11/17		Capt. Playford and Pte. Dauntre proceeded to England on leave.	
do.	9/11/17		Routine Work.	
do.	10/11/17		The D.A.D.V.S. visited the Section and saw animals for evacuation	
do.	11/11/17		Routine Work. Pte. Burrows reported back from VIIth Corps Convalescent Depôt.	
do.	12,13,14/11/17		6 animals were evacuated from MONDICOURT. No. S.E. 11934 Sergt. Evans proceeded from MONDICOURT to ST. POL to undergo a 2 days course on Water Duty at III Army School of Sanitation. Pte. Carter reported back from leave.	

November 1917

51st M.V.S.

Army Form C. 2118.

WAR DIARY
or
INTELLIGENCE SUMMARY.

(Erase heading not required.)

Instructions regarding War Diaries and Intelligence Summaries are contained in F.S. Regs., Part II. and the Staff Manual respectively. Title pages will be prepared in manuscript.

30/11/17

Place	Date	Hour	Summary of Events and Information	Remarks and references to Appendices
WARLINCOURT -LEZ-PAS.	15/11/17		Pte Lee was admitted to 136th Field Ambulance.	
do.	16/11/17		The Section proceeded from WARLINCOURT-LEZ-PAS to MONCHIET.	
do.	17/11/17		Routine Work.	
night of 17/18/16.	10 p.m.		The Section proceeded from MONCHIET to ACHIET-LE-PETIT.	
ACHIET-LE-PETIT.	18/11/17		Routine Work.	
do.	19/11/17		No. S.E.8381 Pte. Boorsma proceeded on leave to England.	
night of 19/20			The Section proceeded from ACHIET-LE-PETIT to BEAULENCOURT and arrived at entrance to LE TRANSLOY. L. Copl. h? Yadgem, Pte. Maddern, Wooldrick's horse whole fair & unknown reported back to please.	
LE TRANSLOY	20/11/17		6 animals were evacuated from ROCQUIGNY.	
do.	21/12nd		Routine Work	
do.	23/11/17		7 animals were evacuated from ROCQUIGNY.	
do.	24/11/17		The Section moved from LE TRANSLOY to ROYALCOURT.	
ROYALCOURT	25/11/17		The A.D.V.S. inspected the Section and inspected animals which had been admitted.	

51st M.V.S.

WAR DIARY or INTELLIGENCE SUMMARY

November 1917

Army Form C. 2118.

Place	Date	Hour	Summary of Events and Information	Remarks and references to Appendices
RUYALCOURT	26/11/17		15 wounded animals were evacuated to IVth Corps Vety Cavalry Clearing Station YTRES. Corpl Playford and Pte Rountree reported back from leave.	
do	27/11/17		Wounded animals were evacuated to IVth Corps Vety C.C.S.	
do	28/11/17	11am	The Section marched from RUYALCOURT to BAPAUME.	
BAPAUME	29/11/17	9am	The Section proceeded from BAPAUME via ACHIET-LE-GRAND, AYETTE-RANSART to BASSEUX.	
BASSEUX	29/11/17		Remounts were received for the Division and distributed to units by the D.A.D.V.S. & O.C. Section.	
do	30/11/17		No. 2715 Pte Nuttall proceeded to England on leave.	

Army Form C. 2118.

WAR DIARY
or
INTELLIGENCE SUMMARY.
(Erase heading not required.)

Instructions regarding War Diaries and Intelligence Summaries are contained in F. S. Regs., Part II. and the Staff Manual respectively. Title pages will be prepared in manuscript.

Place	Date	Hour	Summary of Events and Information	Remarks and references to Appendices
BASSEUX	1/2/17		Nineteen sick animals were handed over to 47th Mobile Veterinary Section, 16th Division at BOIRY-ST RICTRUDE, on the authority of the A.D.V.S., VI Corps, as the Section was standing to, to move.	
"	2/2/17		Routine Work.	
"	3/2/17		The Section marched from BASSEUX to BOIRY-ST RICTRUDE (map reference Sheet 51B S14 C.4.). The animals handed over to the 47th M.V.S. were taken over again and twenty animals were evacuated from BOISLEUX-AU-MONT railhead.	
BOIRY-ST-RICTRUDE	4/2/17		The Section took over from 47th M.V.S., 16th Division. Very good stabling accommodation for the Section horses and sick animals had been erected as well as good billets for officer and men.	
do.	5/2/17		Routine Work.	
do.	6/2/17		No. 12992 Pte. Cornish reported back from leave.	
do.	7/2/17		No. 8381 Pte. Burrows reported back from leave.	
do.	8/2/17		No. 12761 Pte. Baker, A.J. reported for duty from No. 2 Veterinary Hospital and was taken on the strength.	
do.	9/2/17		Sergt. Finch and Pte. Grime proceeded on leave to England.	

A.5834 Wt. W4973/M687 750,000 8/16 D. D. & L. Ltd. Forms/C.2118/13.

WAR DIARY
or
INTELLIGENCE SUMMARY.
(Erase heading not required.)

Army Form C. 2118.

Place	Date	Hour	Summary of Events and Information	Remarks and references to Appendices
BOIRY-ST-RICTRUDE	10/12/17		Animals for evacuation were inspected by the D.A.D.V.S. and 18 animals were evacuated from BOIS LIEUX-DU-MONT.	
do.	11th 12th 13/12/17		Pte. Veale proceeded to VIth Corps School, GIVENCHY-LE-NOBLE to attend the IVth Cookery Class.	
do.	14/12/17		Ophthalmia cases are no longer to be retained on units lines for treatment but have to be sent in to the Section for isolation and treatment or evacuation as decided by the D.A.D.V.S.	
do.	15/12/17		Animals for evacuation were inspected by the D.A.D.V.S.	
do.	16/12/17		Routine work.	
do.	17/12/17		52 Animals were evacuated from BOIS LIEUX-DU-MONT and 23 Ophthalmia cases were discharged cured to their units.	
do.	18 & 19/12/17		Routine work.	
do.	20/12/17		Corps Order No. 1116 received from Base Records. No. 11952 P/F/Sergt Peronn J. is promoted Substantive Sergeant as from 4/12/17. Pte. Nuttall reported back from leave.	

WAR DIARY or INTELLIGENCE SUMMARY

Army Form C. 2118.

Place	Date	Hour	Summary of Events and Information	Remarks and references to Appendices
BOIRY-ST-RICTRUDE.	22/12/17		Routine Work.	
do.	23/12/17		No.12992 Pte. Cornish reported back from leave.	
do.	24/12/17		The D.T.D.V.S. selected ophthalmic cases for discharge. Twenty three cases were returned to their units cured.	
do.	25/12/17		Sergt Inch and Pte. Game reported back from leave. Eighteen animals were evacuated from BOISLEUX-AU-MONT.	
do.	26/12/17		Routine work	
do.	27/12/17 28			
do.	29/12/17		17167 Pte. A. Woodstock was admitted to the 10th Field Ambulance. Pte. Veale reported back from VIth Corps School.	
do.	30/12/17		Routine work.	
do.	31/12/17		The D.T.D.V.S. inspected animals for evacuation. 18 were evacuated including 10 mange cases and 5 ophthalmic cases. 35 ophthalmic cases were selected for discharge to their units.	

M Cameron Capt RVC
O.C. 51 M.V.S.

Army Form C. 2118.

61st Mobile Vet. Section

Vol 20

WAR DIARY
or
INTELLIGENCE SUMMARY.
(Erase heading not required.)

Instructions regarding War Diaries and Intelligence Summaries are contained in F. S. Regs. Part II. and the Staff Manual respectively. Title pages will be prepared in manuscript.

Place	Date	Hour	Summary of Events and Information	Remarks and references to Appendices
BOIRY - ST. MARTIN	1/1/18		Routine work.	
	2/1/18		—— do ——	
	3/1/18		—— do ——	
	4/1/18		—— do ——	
	5/1/18		—— do ——	
	6/1/18		A.A.V.S. inspected ophthalmia cases for discharge, also animals for evacuation	
			No. 25583 Pte GRIMES was admitted to 104 Field Ambulance suffering from myalgia.	
	7/1/18		26 animals were evacuated to No 9 Veterinary Hospital. FORGES-LES-EAUX	
			17 Ophthalmia cases were returned to their units cured.	
			Dvr McKAY. R.F.A. attached to 51 M.V.S. proceeded on leave to England	
	8/1/18		Routine Work	
	9/1/18		—— do ——	
	10/1/18		—— do ——	
	11/1/18		—— do ——	
	12/1/18		—— do ——	
	13/1/18		A.A.R.V.S. inspected animals for evacuation	
	14/1/18		25 animals were evacuated to No 9 Veterinary Hospital. FORGES.	
	15/1/18		11 Ophthalmia cases were discharged to their units cured.	

WAR DIARY
or
INTELLIGENCE SUMMARY.
(Erase heading not required.)

Army Form C. 2118.

Place	Date	Hour	Summary of Events and Information	Remarks and references to Appendices
BOIRY - ST - MARTIN	16/1/18		A.V.C. Personnel of this unit were medically examined for Category A+B men. Routine work	
	17/1/18		— do —	
	18/1/18			
	19/1/18		No. 15014 Pte E.W. ROBERTS reported from No. 2 Veterinary Hospital for duty with 51st M.V.S & was taken on strength accordingly vice Pte S. GRIMES evacuated sick. No. 25207 Pte BARRETT proceeded on R.A.D.V.S. inspected animals for discharge.	
	20/1/18		leave to England. 26 animals were evacuated to No. 7 Veterinary Hospital FORGES. DADVS proceeded on leave to England and Capt G.C. LANCASTER A.V.C. OC 51st Mobile Veterinary Section acts for DADVS during latters absence on leave.	
	21/1/18		15 O.P/Mangey cases were discharged to their units cured. O.C. 51st M.V.S lectured N.C.O.'s, farriers & learners of H.Q. Divisional Train. A.S.C. on the horse's foot and the principles and practice of shoeing.	
	22/1/18		No. 8383 Pte J. ROSSIO reported from No. 6 Veterinary Hospital for duty with Section. OC lectured the Officers of H.Q. Divisional Train A.S.C. on the horses foot + the principles and practice of shoeing.	
	23/1/18		Routine work.	
	24/1/18			
	25/1/18		Pnr. A.J. STONNELL A.S.C. attached + Pte O. OWEN AVC proceeded on leave to England.	
	26/1/18		No. 22808 Pte NEALE proceeded on leave to England.	

Army Form C. 2118.

WAR DIARY
or
INTELLIGENCE SUMMARY.
(Erase heading not required.)

Instructions regarding War Diaries and Intelligence Summaries are contained in F. S. Regs., Part II. and the Staff Manual respectively. Title pages will be prepared in manuscript.

Place	Date	Hour	Summary of Events and Information	Remarks and references to Appendices
BOIRY — ST-MARTIN	27/1/18		As the Lugol treatment for Ophthalmia was found to be causing Opacity of the Eye a 2% solution of normal saline was used instead. This was injected into the lower eyelid by means of a mallein syringe, the dose being 2 c.c.	
	28/1/18		The brood mares of 40th Divn were paraded and branded No 27915 Pte J. NOTTRIL proceeded to No 2 Veterinary Hospital HAVRE to undergo 4 weeks training to fit him for appointment as Sergeant A.V.C. with a field unit. No. 9333/60 Pte J.M. CLOUGH L.IV. proceeded on leave to England	
	29/1/18		O.C. lectured N.C.O.s and men of 40th D divisional train A.S.C. on the diseases of the horses foot	
	30/1/18		30 animals were evacuated to No 9 Veterinary Hospital FORGES. O.O. lectured Officers of 40th Divnl train A.S.C. on diseases of the horse's foot.	
	31/1/18		Routine work.	

FEBRUARY 1918.

WAR DIARY
or
INTELLIGENCE SUMMARY.

Army Form C. 2118.

51 M&V Vety Sec

Place	Date	Hour	Summary of Events and Information	Remarks and references to Appendices
BOIRY ST. MARTIN.	1/2/18		Eighteen Ophthalmia cases were discharged to units.	
do	2nd & 3rd		Routine work.	
"	4/2/18		19 animals were evacuated from BOISLEUX-AU-MONT.	
"	5/2/18		Pte. Barrett reported back from leave.	
"	6/2/18		Routine work.	
"	8/2/18		Animals for evacuation were inspected by the D.A.D.V.S.	
"	9/2/18		Routine work.	
"	10/2/18		Capt. Lancaster, O.C. Mobile Section proceeded on leave to England and Capt. P. Haigh, V.O. ℅ 178 Bde., R.F.A. took over command of the Section	
"	11/2/18		The D.A.D.V.S. marked animals for evacuation and 37 were evacuated from BOISLEUX-AU-MONT. Pre Shorvell, A.S.C. and Pte. Owen reported back from leave.	
"	12/2/18		A memo was received from D.A.D.V.S. that treatment of Specific Ophthalmia with Lugol's Solution was to be suspended and Atropine in Vaseline (1%) was to be tried and results reported on. The ointment to be placed within the eyelids.	
"	13/2/18		The new method of preparing evacuation rolls is to be continued, shews the rolls simply shows serial case number of animal, its class, disease + unit.	

WAR DIARY or INTELLIGENCE SUMMARY

Army Form C. 2118.

28/3/18

Place	Date	Hour	Summary of Events and Information	Remarks and references to Appendices
BOIRY ST. MARTIN	14/3/18		In accordance with instructions received the men of the Section are being given 15 minutes daily exercise in gas drill. Instructions were also received that those men of the Section who had not previously undergone instruction in musketry were to go through a course.	
"	15/3/18		Sergt. J.H. Wilson of 13th Yorks Regt. reported for duty as Musketry Instructor	
"	16/3/18	9.30 am	The musketry course started. Fourteen men have to take the course and fire about 50 rounds.	
"	17/3/18		Animals for evacuation were inspected by the DADVS. No. 14734 Pte. Evans proceeded on leave.	
"	18/3/18		31 animals were evacuated from BOISLEUX-AU-MONT.	
"	19/3/18		No. 11852 Sergt. Brown proceeded on leave.	
"	20/3/18		AVC Orders No. 15 dated 16/3/18 was received from DADVS. In the no. 15341 Pte. McFadyean is appointed paid acting Corporal.	
"	21/3/18 22/3/18 23/3/18 24/3/18		Routine work The DADVS inspected animals for evacuation	

Army Form C. 2118.

WAR DIARY
or
INTELLIGENCE SUMMARY.
(Erase heading not required.)

28/7/18

Place	Date	Hour	Summary of Events and Information	Remarks and references to Appendices
BOIRY-ST- MARTIN	25/7/18		32 animals were evacuated from BOISLEUX-DU-MONT	
"	26/7/18		Routine Work	
"	27/7/18		Movement Order for the Section was received from the 3/A.D.V.S.	
"	28/7/18	3pm	The Section proceeded to BELLACOURT via PONFER and RANSART. No 9355 Corpl. Hopkin was left in charge of Sick animals for evacuation which were to be handed over to incoming Mobile	

Peter Henry/Cpt MR

WR

Army Form C. 2118.

51 M.V.S. 40D
WAR DIARY
INTELLIGENCE SUMMARY.
(Erase heading not required.)

March 1918.

Instructions regarding War Diaries and Intelligence Summaries are contained in F.S. Regs., Part II. and the Staff Manual respectively. Title pages will be prepared in manuscript.

Place	Date	Hour	Summary of Events and Information	Remarks and references to Appendices
BELLACOURT	1st 2nd /3/18		Routine Work.	
do.	3rd		The Section marched from BELLACOURT to MONCHIET. Eight sick animals were handed over to 144th Mobile Vet. Section 34th Division who took over at BOIRY-ST-RICTRUDE and the N.C.O. left in charge of these rejoined the Section.	
MONCHIET	4th		No. 17167 Pte. Woolcock, A.V.C. proceeded to 137th Field Ambulance at BAILLEULMONT to undergo a course in Sanitary Duties.	
do.	5th		No. 26446 Pte. Warner proceeded to England on leave.	
do.	6th		Twenty-nine animals were evacuated from BEAUMETZ-RIVIÈRE. A Board of Officers, President Captain Conan Royilant 40th Divnl. from A.S.C. reviewed the equipment of the Section.	
do.	7th 8th		The NCOs and men of the Section who had not previously been through a musketry course fired a course of 50 rounds on the range at BASSEUX. Sergt Brown and Corpl Evans reported back from leave.	
do.	9th		Routine Work.	
do.	10th		The D.A.D.V.S. accompanied by the A.A & Q.M.G. of the Division Lt. Col. Moores Cmdg. D.S.O. inspected the Section and animals for evacuation	

* 51 M.V.S. *

Army Form C. 2118.

March 1918.

WAR DIARY
— or —
INTELLIGENCE SUMMARY.
(Erase heading not required.)

Instructions regarding War Diaries and Intelligence Summaries are contained in F. S. Regs., Part II. and the Staff Manual respectively. Title pages will be prepared in manuscript.

Place	Date	Hour	Summary of Events and Information	Remarks and references to Appendices
MONCHIET	10th		No.25707 Pte. Barrett, A.V.C. reported to 137th Field Ambulance at BAILLEUMONT to undergo a course of instruction in water duties	
do.	11th		Twenty four animals were evacuated from BEAUMETZ-RIVIÈRE.	
do.	12th		No. 220 S. Sergt. Westwood proceeded to England on one month's leave of absence on expiration of his army engagement.	
do.	13th		Twelve animals were evacuated from BEAUMETZ-RIVIÈRE and the Section marched to HENDECOURT	
HENDECOURT	14th		Orders were received to stand by to move at 1½ hours notice.	
do.	15th 16th		Routine work.	
do	17th		Animals for evacuation were inspected by the A.D.V.S. Private Roberts reported back from leave, his leave having been extended by 3 days by Officer i/c A.V.C. Home Records.	
do.	18th		Nine animals were evacuated from BOILEUX-AU-MONT.	
do.	19th 20th 21st		Routine work	
do.	22nd		Some men of the Section were sent to wagon lines of 181 Bde., R.F.A. at HAMELINCOURT to collect horses wounded in the opening bombardment of the battle. No. 22808 Pte. Veale, A.V.C. proceeded to VI Corps Sinking Bath MON DICOURT.	

March 1918.

51 M.V.S.

WAR DIARY
or
INTELLIGENCE SUMMARY.
(Erase heading not required.)

Army Form C. 2118.

Place	Date	Hour	Summary of Events and Information	Remarks and references to Appendices
HEBUTERNE	22nd	4pm	An urgent message was received for the Section to move to ADINFER.	
do.	do.	6pm.	The Section marched to ADINFER.	
ADINFER	23rd		Six wounded animals which were incurably injured were destroyed.	
"	24th		The Section marched to HANNES CAMP.	
"	25th		Twenty two animals were evacuated from LA HERLIÈRE. Orders were received to move to ST AMAN II.	
"	26th		The Section moved to ST. AMAN II, & thence to MEZERELLES	
"	27th		The Section returned to ST. AMAN II	
"	28th		The Section marched from ST AMAND to HUMBERCOURT. 15 animals were evacuated from SAULTY.	
HUMBERCOURT	29th	10am.	The Section moved from HUMBERCOURT to HERLIN-LE-VERT near CHELERS.	
HERLIN-LE-VERT.	30th	9am.	The Section rested here for the day.	
do.	31st	9am.	The Section proceeded from HERLIN-LE-VERT to LILLERS via BRUAY.	

G. Gloucester Capt. A.V.C.
O.C. 51 M.V.S.
2/4/18

51st MOBILE VETERINARY SECTION

WAR DIARY or INTELLIGENCE SUMMARY

APRIL 1918

MAP REFERENCE. HAZEBROUCK. 5A.

Army Form C. 2118.

Place	Date	Hour	Summary of Events and Information	Remarks and references to Appendices
LILLERS	1/4/18		The Section proceeded to TROU·BAYARD via MERVILLE and ESTAIRES.	
TROU·BAYARD	2/4/18		The Section took over from the 2/1st West Lancs. M.V.S, 57th Division. There was very good accommodation for a Mobile Section; covered standings for all animals including isolation cases.	
do.	3/4/18		The D.A.D.V.S. visited the Section and inspected animals for evacuation. Nine animals were evacuated to XVth Corps Veterinary Evacuation Station LA·GORGUE	
do.	4/4/18			
do.	5/4/18		The D.A.D.V.S. inspected the animals for evacuation. Twenty three animals were sent to XVth Corps V.E.S. and also six men of the Section for attachment.	
do.	6/4/18		Routine Work.	
do.	7/4/18			
do.	8/4/18	4 a.m	Battle of ARMENTIÈRES commenced. Owing to heavy shelling the Section received orders to proceed to VIEUX·BERQUIN.	
		9.30 a.m	The Section proceeded to VIEUX·BERQUIN and arrived at 4 p.m, as this place was being shelled the Section proceeded to RUE·DE·BOIS.	
RUE·DE·BOIS	9th to 10/4/18		Routine Work.	
do.	11/4/18		Twenty two animals were evacuated to XVth Corps V.E.S. Orders were received to move with 40th Divnl Train to BORRE. The Section proceeded to BORRE, joined No 9 Coy, A.S.C. and proceeded to BORRE.	

51st MOBILE VETERINARY SECTION

WAR DIARY or INTELLIGENCE SUMMARY.

Army Form C. 2118.

APRIL 1918

Place	Date	Hour	Summary of Events and Information	Remarks and references to Appendices
BORRE.	12/4/18.		The Section moved with No. 2 Army, A.S.C. from BORRE to HONDEGHEM.	
HONDEGHEM.	13/4/18.		Ten animals were evacuated to XVth Corps V.E.S.	
do.	14/4/18.		The Section moved to LONGUENESSE via ST. OMER. No. 202 S. Sergt. Westwood returned back from leave.	
LONGUENESSE	15/4/18.		Routine work.	
do.	16/4/18.		A stock-taking was made of equipment, and anything in recent operations was indented for.	
do.	17/4/18.		Nine animals were evacuated direct to No. 23 Veterinary Hospital, ST. OMER.	
do.	18th/19th		Routine Work.	
do.	20/4/18		Capt. S. Hunter, A.V.C.(S.R.) arrived to take over command of the Section from Capt. G.C. Lancaster, A.V.C.(S.R.).	
do.	21/4/18.		Captain S. Hunter, A.V.C.(S.R.) took over command of the Section in place of Captain G.C. Lancaster. Ten animals were evacuated direct to No. 23 Veterinary Hospital, ST. OMER. No. S.E.1202 Pte. Harvey reported for duty from No. 2 Veterinary Hospital, HAVRE and was taken on the strength.	
		2.30 p.m.	The Section proceeded to BOISDINGHEM and was billetted in the 119th Inf. Bde. area.	

51st MOBILE VETERINARY
WAR DIARY SECTION
or
INTELLIGENCE SUMMARY.

APRIL 1918.

Army Form C. 2118.

Place	Date	Hour	Summary of Events and Information	Remarks and references to Appendices
BRISDING-HEM	22/4/18		No. S.E. 15341 Pte. McFadyean was despatched to No. 9 Vety Hospital, HAVRE for training as a Sergt. D.V.C. to a field Unit.	
do.	23/4/18		No. S.E. 14104 Pte. Ers. Roberts was despatched to No. 9 Vety Hospital HAVRE, for transfer to England for farming, in accordance with instructions received from D.A.G's Office.	
do.	24/27th		Routine Work.	
do.	28th		Animals for evacuation were inspected by D.A.D.V.S.	
do.	29th		Ten animals were evacuated direct to No. 23 Vety Hospital ST OMER. Orders were received from D.D.V.S. to send for 5 men of the Section who were attached to XV th Corps Veterinary Evacuation Station. Orders were received for the Section to be ready to move to-morrow 30th inst.	
do.	30th		The Section marched to SENINGHEM (130th Inf. Bde. area).	

COMMANDING 51st MOBILE VETY. SECTION.

Army Form C. 2118.

51st M.V.S.

WAR DIARY
or
INTELLIGENCE SUMMARY.

MAY 1918

Place	Date	Hour	Summary of Events and Information	Remarks and references to Appendices
SENINGHEM Map Reference: HAZEBROUCK 5A— (A) 4.	1st 2nd		Routine work.	
do.	3rd		Three animals were evacuated by road to No. 23 Veterinary Hospital, ST OMER.	
do.	4th		The Section moved by road to ST MOMELIN (Map reference: HAZEBROUCK 5A— (II) 3.) via SETQUES, LONGUENESSE and ST OMER. No. 14,2759 Driver McKay was despatched from the Section (to which he had been attached) to rejoin his unit, No.1 Section 40th A.A.C. A memo was received from Officer i/c Records saying that owing to the formation of Veterinary Evacuation Stations, the War Establishment of the Section was to be reduced by 1 Staff Sergeant and 6 Privates; the A.V.C. personnel, other ranks to be 18 instead of 25.	
ST MOMELIN Map ref HAZEBROUCK 5A— (II) 3.	5th		Animals for evacuation were inspected by the D.A.D.V.S. and were evacuated by road to No. 23 Vety Hospital, ST OMER. No. 37988 Pte. O. Owen of the 7th Welsh Regiment, who had been attached to the Section was also despatched to rejoin his unit.	

Army Form C. 2118.

May 1918

WAR DIARY
or
INTELLIGENCE SUMMARY.
(Erase heading not required.)

Instructions regarding War Diaries and Intelligence Summaries are contained in F. S. Regs., Part II. and the Staff Manual respectively. Title pages will be prepared in manuscript.

Place	Date	Hour	Summary of Events and Information	Remarks and references to Appendices
ST.MOMELIN.	6th		Eight animals were evacuated by road to No 23 Vety Hospital, ST OMER.	
do.	7th		Routine Work.	
do.	8th		Message Carrying Dogs (Signal Service) are now to be received by mobile Veterinary Sections and evacuated in the same manner as horses or mules (D.V.S. Circular memo. 232). Their daily ration consists of 8 lb. Broken bread or biscuit and 1/2 lb. Horseflesh.	
do.	9th		Four animals were evacuated by road to No. 23 Vety Hospital, ST OMER.	
do.	10th		Six animals were evacuated to ST OMER.	
do.	11th		The Section marched to LE TOM (map reference Sheet 27 – 1.33.c.3.3.)	
LE.TOM Sht 27 1.33.c.3.3.	12th		No. 30286 Pte. C.L. Adams, A.V.C., reported for duty from No. 12 Vety Hospital, and was taken on the strength.	
do.	13th		Routine Work.	
do.	14th		The D.P.D.V.S. inspected the Section. Two animals were evacuated by road to ST OMER. One H.D. horse, surplus to establishment, was handed over to Divnl H.Q.	
do.	15th 16th 17th		Routine Work.	
do.	18th		No. SE. 5984 Sergt. J.H. Warton, A.V.C., who was attached to the S.P.A. Section, A.C.A R.A.C., and most surplus reported for temporary attachment to the Section —	

WAR DIARY
or
INTELLIGENCE SUMMARY.
(Erase heading not required.)

Army Form C. 2118.

May 1918

Place	Date	Hour	Summary of Events and Information	Remarks and references to Appendices
LE TOM^t.	19th		A memo. was received from the D.A.D.V.S. re: the treatment of horses affected by mustard gas. These are to be treated at once with chloride of lime, either rubbed on dry to the affected parts, then washed off both with soap and water or used in the form of a solution, 1 lb. of chloride of lime being mixed with water to form a paste and then 4 gallons of water added gradually -	
do.	20th		15 animals were evacuated direct to No. 23 Vet^y Hospital, ST. OMER.	
do.	21st 22nd		Routine Work.	
do.	23rd		No. 98224 Pte S.G. Temple of 114th Labour Coy. reported for 10 days' attachment to be tested as to his suitability for transfer to the A.V.C. No. S.E. 5984 Sergt. J.H. Warton was despatched to No. 2 Vet^y Hospital, HAVRE.	
do.	24th		Routine Work.	
do.	25th		No. S.E. 17167 Pte A. Woodstock, A.V.C. was appointed Acting Corporal.	
do.	26th 27th		Routine Work.	
do.			14 animals were evacuated to ST. OMER. 1 animal (of 705th Labour Coy) suffering from farcine, died.	
do.	28th		A memo. was received from the D.A.D.V.S. saying no animal of the French Army suffering from EPIZOOTIC LYMPHANGITIS is to be sent in for evacuation. Then animals so affected have inadvertently be admitted and not removed until a reasonable time by the French Authorities after they had been informed, it should be destroyed -	

WAR DIARY
or
INTELLIGENCE SUMMARY

Army Form C. 2118.

Place	Date	Hour	Summary of Events and Information	Remarks and references to Appendices
LE TM.	29th 30th 31st		Routine Work. During the month opportunity has been afforded to bring the equipment of the Section up to War Establishment and for the overhaul of vehicles and other equipment.	
			APPENDIX. Statement of Sick Animals Received & thus disposed of.	

Admitted   68

Evacuated   61
Died   2
Destroyed   nil
Missing   nil
Remaining   5
            ___
Total   68.

Evacuated
Debility   20
Mange   13
Wound (Antero) 5
Ulcer. Cellulitis 3
Injuries   16
Surgical Condition 4
            ___
Total   61

Died
Enteritis (Acute) 1
Jaundice   1

Remaining
Sore back   1
Ulcer. Cellulitis 2
Ringworm   1
Strangles   1
                ___
Total   5

O.C. 57 M.V.S
31/5/18.

51st M.V.S.

June 1918

Vol 25

WAR DIARY
INTELLIGENCE SUMMARY

Army Form C. 2118.

Place	Date	Hour	Summary of Events and Information	Remarks and references to Appendices
LE TOM. Sheet 27- H3d.	1/6/18.		No. 222 Staff Sergt Westwood proceeded to No. 24 Veterinary Hospital. The A.D.V.S. VIIth Corps, accompanied by the D.A.D.V.S., Division, inspected the Section. Six animals were evacuated by road to No. 23 Vety Hospital, ST OMER.	
	2nd 3rd 4th 5th		Routine work. One float case was evacuated to No. 23 Vety Hospital.	
	6th		The new War Establishment for the Section was received from the D.D.V.S. The horse strength is reduced by four riders, the horse strength of the Section is now to be eleven riders and four light draught.	
	7th 8th		Routine work.	
	9th		Owing to reduction of the A.V.C. personnel of the Section six privates who became surplus, were despatched to No. 2 Veterinary Hospital, HAVRE. These men were Nos. 30286 Pte. C.L. Adams, 11680 Pte. E. Seery, 1202 Pte. S. Harvey, 22706 Pte. J. Semple, 11727 Pte. J. Smith, and 26446 Pte. J.E. Warner.	
	11th		Three animals were evacuated to No. 23 Vety Hospital, ST OMER.	
	12th		One float case was evacuated to No. 23 Vety Hospital.	
	13th		A hand clipper fitted with a new tin protector arrived at the Section for trial.	
	15th		Orders were received from D.D.V.S. for the Section to proceed on the 16th inst. to ST MOMELIN.	
	16th		The Section marched to ST MOMELIN.	

Army Form C. 2118.

WAR DIARY
INTELLIGENCE SUMMARY.
(Erase heading not required.)

Instructions regarding War Diaries and Intelligence Summaries are contained in F. S. Regs., Part II. and the Staff Manual respectively. Title pages will be prepared in manuscript.

Place	Date	Hour	Summary of Events and Information	Remarks and references to Appendices
ST. MOMELIN	17th		Two animals were evacuated to ST. OMER. (No. 23 Vety Hospital)	
Mah HAZEBROUCK 5A	18th		Three animals were evacuated.	
	M/Zoth 21st		Routine Work	
(D)3	22nd		Notification was received from the D.A.D.V.S. that No. S.E. 9049 Sergt. J. Finch has been awarded the Meritorious Service Medal. Two animals were evacuated. The D.A.D.V.S. saw the hand clippers with new tin protector in use. This protector does not interfere with the clipping and appears to be a good protector for the teeth of the rotation.	
	23rd		Orders were received for the Section to proceed to LYNDE. The Section marched to LYNDE.	
LYNDE Ref 36A C11 a 4.4	25th		The A.D.V.S. XV Corps visited the Section.	
	26th		One Section Rides (mules) were vanned to Capt J.R. Rigby R.V.C.	
	28th		Three animals were evacuated to No. 15 Veterinary Evacuation Station.	
	29th		The D.A.D.V.S. inspected the animals for evacuation	
	30th		Three animals were evacuated to No. 15 Veterinary Evac Station.	

P.T.O.

WAR DIARY
or
INTELLIGENCE SUMMARY

Army Form C. 2118.

Place	Date	Hour	Summary of Events and Information	Remarks and references to Appendices
			Appendix. Statement of Sick Animals received & evacuated &c.	

Remaining from last month 5
Admitted June 29
Total 34

Evacuated 30
Died nil
Destroyed nil
Saved as Remounts 2
Remaining 2
Total 34

EVACUATIONS

Class 1 Debility ---- 2
Class 2 Pneumonia ---- 1
Class 9 Mange ---- 1
         Neo Derm ---- } 1½ (?)
Class 10 Ringbone 2 } 4
         Spavin 1 }
         Splint 1 }
Class 11 Ulcer. Cellulitis ---- 4
Class 12 Opth. & Blind ---- 4
Class 13 Contusions 2 }
         Sore Back 2 } 13
         P.U.N. 3 }
         Shrapnel & G.S. 2 }
         Kicks 4 }

Total 30

S. Hunt
Capt. R.V.C.
O.C. 51 M.V.S.

51st MOBILE VETERINARY SECTION.

WAR DIARY

INTELLIGENCE SUMMARY

(Erase heading not required.)

Army Form C. 2118

July 1918

Place	Date	Hour	Summary of Events and Information	Remarks and references to Appendices
LYNDE Map Reference Sheet 36A B.11.a.6.4.	1st		Routine Work	
	2nd		Two animals were evacuated to No.15 Veterinary Evacuation Station.	
	3rd		Routine work	
	4th		Three animals were evacuated to No.15 V.E.S. One Officer's Veterinary Chest (Bulls) and 4 wallets, surplus owing to reduction of veterinary equipment, were despatched to No.2 Advanced Base of Veterinary Stores.	
do.	5th		Routine Work	
do.	6th		No.Z/065334 Driver Stonnell, A.S.C., attached to the Section, reported back for duty from No.2 Australian C.C.S.	
do.	8th		One animal was evacuated to No.15 V.E.S.	
do.	10th		The D.A.D.V.S. inspected the Section. Two animals were evacuated to No.15 V.E.S and one was discharged to its unit (10th Bn. K.O.S.Bor[de]rs) cured.	
do.	11th		The A.D.V.S. XVth Corps inspected the Section.	
do.	13th		Anti-tetanic serum is not being used until further orders in accordance with instructions of D.V.S.	
do.	14th		One animal, with fractured radius, was destroyed	

2.

Army Form C. 2118

51st M.V.S.
WAR DIARY
INTELLIGENCE SUMMARY
July 1918

(Erase heading not required.)

Place	Date	Hour	Summary of Events and Information	Remarks and references to Appendices
LYNDE	15th		The carcase of the animal destroyed was sent to BUCHERIE ECONOMIQUE at AIRE.	
do.	16th		The G.O.C., 40th Division, Major General Sir W.E. Peyton, K.C.B, K.C.V.O., D.S.O., accompanied by the A.A. & Q.M.G., Lt. Col. C.J. Moores, C.M.G., D.S.O., and the G.S.O.I, Lt. Col. Black, D.S.O., inspected the Section. The D.A.D.V.S., 40th Division, Major W.N. Rawdon, accompanied the G.O.C. Also, Horses, vehicles, harness, pharmacy, billets and cook-house were inspected. The G.O.C. expressed himself quite satisfied with the cleanliness and general appearance of the Section, which, he said, he would visit again.	
do.	17th		Three animals were evacuated to No. 15 V.E.S. One horse was received from the French Army.	
do.	18th		Five animals were evacuated to No. 15 V.E.S.	
do.	19th		Four animals (including one from the French Army) were evacuated to No. 15 V.E.S.	
do.	20th		No. T.O/5 33k Driver Shonell, A.S.C., attached to the Section was awarded 21 days No. 1 Field Punishment for using threatening and insubordinate language to an N.C.O. One animal was discharged and to its unit (135th Field Ambulance)	

51st M.V.S.
WAR DIARY
or
INTELLIGENCE SUMMARY
(Erase heading not required.)

July 1918

Army Form C. 2118

3.

Place	Date	Hour	Summary of Events and Information	Remarks and references to Appendices
LYNDE.	21st		The D.A.D.V.S. inspected the Section. From to-day the hay ration is reduced by 1 lb.	
do.	22nd		One animal was discharged cured to its unit (23rd Bn. Cheshire Regt)	
do.	23rd		Four animals were evacuated to No. 15 V.E.S.	
do.	24th 25th		Routine Work	
"	26th		One animal was evacuated to No. 15 V.E.S.	
"	29th		Four animals were evacuated to No. 15 V.E.S.	
"	30th		One float case was evacuated direct to No. 23 Vety. Hospital, STOMER.	
"	31st		do	
			During the month earth traverses 2'6" high and 2' broad have been built round tents and horse standings as a protection against bombs dropped.	

51st M.V.S.
WAR DIARY
INTELLIGENCE SUMMARY

July 1918 — Army Form C. 2118

Statement of Animals received during the month and how disposed of.

Remaining from last month ----- 2
Admitted ----- 44
Total ----- 46

Evacuated ----- 33
Destroyed ----- 1
Discharged to units ----- 3
Shed ----- 9
Remaining -----
Total ----- 46

EVACUATED.

Class I   Debility 2

Class 9.
  Neo. Dermatitis --- 5
  Mange --- 1

Class 10.
  Sorebacks
  Ringbones --- 1

Class 12.
  Blind Cataracts --- 3
  " Shokht?
  Anaemia --- 3

Class 13.
  Wd. contd (Kick)
  "   "   (bite)
  " Animal
  Abscess
  Sore Back
  Spr. Engorment

Class 11
  West
  Cellulitis 2

O.C. 51/M.V.S.

51st MOBILE VETERINARY SECTION
WAR DIARY or INTELLIGENCE SUMMARY

Army Form C. 2118

August 1918

Place	Date	Hour	Summary of Events and Information	Remarks and references to Appendices
LYNDE Sheet 36A B.11.a.6.4	1/8/18		One animal of 19th Worcestershire Regt, suffering from fractured tibia, was destroyed.	
	2nd		One animal was evacuated to No. 23 Vety Hospital, ST OMER and 3 animals were evacuated to No. 15 Vety Evacuation Station.	
	3rd		One H.D. horse of 9th Heavy Battery, R.G.A., suffering from fractured tibia was seen at M. BOIDIN, Rue de ST OMER, AIRE, and then destroyed.	
	4th 5/9th		Animals for evacuation were inspected by the D.A.D.V.S. Routine Work.	
	10th		The D.A.D.V.S. inspected animals for evacuation and also Section horses entered for the Divisional Horse Show.	
	11th		Three animals were evacuated to No. 15 V.E.S. No. S.E. 257/18 Pte. E. Hawthorn proceeded on leave to England.	
	12th		One float case was evacuated to No. 23 Vety Hospital, ST OMER.	
	13th		Four animals were evacuated to No. 15 V.E.S.	
	14th		One animal was discharged cured to its unit (13th Royal Innoskelling Fusiliers)	
	15th		A.V.C. Local Orders No. 81 was received confirming the appointment of No. S.E. 1967 Pte. A. Woodstock to the rank of P/A/Corpl to complete to War establishment.	
	16th		One animal was evacuated to No. 15 V.E.S.	

2

51st M.V.S.

WAR DIARY
or
INTELLIGENCE SUMMARY

Army Form C. 2118

August 1918

Place	Date	Hour	Summary of Events and Information	Remarks and references to Appendices
LYNDE,	14th		One animal (Hot case) was evacuated to No. 23 Vet'y Hospital, ST. OMER.	
	18th		No. S.E. 5940 S. Smith R. Barefoot proceeded on leave to England.	
	19th		The Brunt Horse Show took place near RENESCURE (Sh. 127 – T29). In the stripped horse events (L.D. and R class) the Section won 1st prize in each event and also 2nd prize in N.C.O. jumping.	
	20th		One animal was discharged to its unit (23rd Bn. Loires Fusiliers)	
	21st		The 3 Section brood mares were shown for inspection at BAVINCHOVE – (27/0.15d.5.1)	
	22nd		One animal (flot case) was evacuated to No. 23 Vet'y Hospital, ST. OMER.	
	23rd		One animal was evacuated to No. 15 V.E.S. –	
	24th		The Section moved to ST. LEGER (Sheet 36A – C.2.c.3.3.) and took over billet from A1st M.V.S., 31st Division –	
ST-LEGER 36A-C.2.C.33	25th		The D.A.D.V.S. inspected the Section; One animal was evacuated to No. 15 V.E.S.	
	26th		No. 15019 Pte. C. Carter proceeded to England on leave – Capt. S. Hunter, A.V.C., prior to proceeding on leave, handed over charge of Section to Capt. J.R. Rigby, A.V.C.	
	27th		Capt. J.R. Rigby took command of the Section –	
	29th		No. S.E. 30426 Pte. G. Grinstead reported from No. 2 Convalescent Horse Depot for duty and No. S.E. 25718 Pte. V.E. Flintham reported back from leave.	

51/M.V.S.

WAR DIARY
or
INTELLIGENCE SUMMARY   Army Form C. 2118

August 1918

(Erase heading not required.)

Place	Date	Hour	Summary of Events and Information	Remarks and references to Appendices
ST. LEGER	30th		The D.A.D.V.S. inspected animals for evacuation. Sick animals were evacuated to no. 15 V.E.S. The Section moved to Sheet 27/U 30 b 22 (near WAILON-CAPPEL.)	
U.30 b.32.	31st		No. S.F. 4934 Pte. D.A. Evans proceeded to no. 2 Veterinary Hospital, HAVRE.	
Appendix			Statement of Animals received during month & how disposed of.	

Remaining from last month --- 9
Admitted --- 31
Total --- 40

Disposal
Evacuated --- 31
Destroyed --- 2
Returned cured to Units --- 4
Remaining --- 3
Total --- 40

Evacuated

Class 1 Rabies --- 1
Class 8 Radial paralysis --- 1
Class 10. Aphtha 3
          Lipthema 1
          Strain 1
Class 11 Membitis 2
Class 12 Blind --- 3

Class 13
Wd. Contd.(Fet.) 2
" Shell fnd 2
" Lacerated 3
" contd 4
" punctd 2
Saddle gall 1
Rope gall 1
Abscess 1
Pumplet hole 1
Sp. tendons 1
Dislocation 1
Fistula 1

R. Knapp Capt. A.V.C.
O.C. 51 M.V.S.

51 M.V.S.

Sept 1918

WAR DIARY
or
INTELLIGENCE SUMMARY

Army Form C. 2118.

Place	Date	Hour	Summary of Events and Information	Remarks and references to Appendices
Sheet 27 V.30.c.2.2.	1st/2nd		Routine Work.	
	3rd		Seven animals were evacuated to No. 15 Veterinary Evacuation Station	
	4th		The Section moved to LE FARRA D.S. near VIEUX-BERQUIN (Sheet 36 S.11.a.2.2.) No. S.E. 59.40 S. Enitch Banefront reported back from leave.	
Sheet 36 R E.11.a.2.4	5th		The D & D.V.S. inspected the Section.	
	6th		The Horse Ambulance in charge of Sgt Shonnell A.S.C. arrived to No 4 Ordnance Mobile Workshop (Heavy) at ESQUELBECQUE for repair.	
	7th/8th		Routine work	
	9th		Six animals were evacuated to No. 15 Vety Evacuation Station. Notice was received from A.P.O. at HAZEBROUCK (Sheet 27 - V.29.d.2.4) that No. S.E. 15019 Pte C. Carter whilst on leave had been admitted to No. 14 London General Hospital.	
	10th/11th		The Horse Ambulance was sent for and returned to the Section	
	12th		Capt. S. Hunter returned from leave and took over command of the Section from Capt J.R. Rigby. D.A.D.V.S. inspected animals for evacuation and seven animals were evacuated to No. 15 Vety Evacuation Station (Advanced Pool)	

SIMVS

WAR DIARY / Sept 1918

INTELLIGENCE SUMMARY.

Army Form C. 2118.

Place	Date	Hour	Summary of Events and Information	Remarks and references to Appendices
	13/14th		Routine Work	
	15th		Nine animals were evacuated to No.15 Vety. Evacuation Station.	
	16th		During the absence of Major Wm Ruston, A.V.C., D.A.D.V.S., Capt. S. Dunlop, O.C. Section acted for him	
	18th		Seven animals were evacuated to No.15 Vety. Evacuation Station	
	20th		No.9049 Sergt. Trick proceeded from BAILLEUL to CALAIS with a party to draw remounts for the Division.	
	21st		No.17167 Corpl. A. Woodstock proceeded on leave to England. Six animals were evacuated to No. 15 Vety. Evacuation Station	
	22nd		Seven animals were evacuated to No.15 V.E.S. Two mules were admitted suffering from gas poisoning (both flash cases). Parts of the body which went level protected by hair (eye, muzzle, anal and perineal regions) were very severely affected. They were both evacuated as float cases.	
	23rd/24th		Routine Work	
	25th		Seven animals were evacuated to No.15 Veterinary Evacuation Station	
	26th		Three animals were evacuated to No.15 V.E.S. No. 14984 Pte. H. Madden proceeded to England on leave.	

51 MVS
Sept 1918

3

Army Form C. 2118.

WAR DIARY
or
INTELLIGENCE SUMMARY.

(Erase heading not required.)

Place	Date	Hour	Summary of Events and Information	Remarks and references to Appendices
	28th		No. 1310 Pte J. Horsick reported for duty from No. 2 Veterinary Hospital. The rifles and gas helmets of the Section were inspected. Two animals were evacuated to No. 15 Veterinary Evacuation Station. The A.D.V.S. XV Corps inspected the Section.	
	29th		Six animals were evacuated to No. 15 V.E.S.	
	30th		Ten animals were evacuated to No. 15 Veterinary Evacuation Station.	

APPENDIX — P.T.O.

51 M.V.S.

WAR DIARY
or
INTELLIGENCE SUMMARY.

Army Form C. 2118.

Sept 1919.

(Erase heading not required.)

Place	Date	Hour	Summary of Events and Information	Remarks and references to Appendices

APPENDIX:-

Statement of number of Animals received during the month & how disposed of

		Evacuated	
No. remaining from last month	3	Class I	
No. Admitted 1/30 Sept 1919	92	" II	Debility 19
Total	95	" 9	Strongyles 1
			Mange 3 — 4
No. Evacuated	85		Wounds Nematodes
No. Died	nil		Sitfast 1
No. Destroyed	1		Ringbone 1 — 3
Nature of discharge of limb	3	" 10	Swelled 1
Strayed/escaped/Slaughtered/received	3	" 11	Mal. ulcers 3
		" 12	Blood (Anyroroid)
	92		Sp. Chlikalmia } 12
Remaining on 30th Sept	3	" 13	Wd contd. Kick 8
Total	95		" Lacerated 4
			" Punctured 5
			" Shell 12
			" Bomb 5 — 43
			Gas poisoning 2
			Sp. Argamenk 3
			P.J.N. 1
			Abscess 1
			Sore back 1
			Mud rash sore 1
			Total 85

Army Form C. 2118.

WAR DIARY
or
INTELLIGENCE SUMMARY.
(Erase heading not required.)

M.V. Section

Place	Date	Hour	Summary of Events and Information	Remarks and references to Appendices
LE PARADIS SW 36ᴬ F.19.9.2.4.	1/10/18		Routine work.	
	2/10/18		—do—	
	3/10/18		No 19761 Pte Baker. A. proceeded to England on leave. 4 Animals were evacuated to 15 Vety Evac Stn	
			3 Animals were evacuated to 15 V.E.S.	
	4/10/18		An advance party was sent on to reoccupy billets at SW 36A/B 30 b 2.8.	
STEENWERCK. 36ᴬ B 30 b 2.8.	5/10/18		The Section marched to STEENWERCK. Sheet 36ᴬ B 30 b 2.8.	
	6/10/18		Routine work.	
	7/10/18		Animals for Evacuation were inspected by D.A.D.V.S.	
	8/10/18.		7 Animals evacuated to 15 Vety Evacuation Station advanced post at Sheet 27. W 24 d. 0.5.	
			No 10473. Corpl Playford. J. proceeded to England on leave.	
			No 17167. Corpl Woolstock A. reported back from leave to England	
	9/10/18		Routine work.	
	10/10/18		— do —	
	11/10/18		— do —	
	12/10/18		10 Animals evacuated to 15 V.E.S.	
	13/10/18		Routine work	
	14/10/18		— do —	
	15/10/18		— do —	
	16/10/18		14 Animals evacuated to 15·V·E·S	
	17/10/18		A mule admitted to Section from Army troops R.E. died. Postmortem examination revealed cause of death to be Enteritis.	
ARMENTIERES.	18/10/18		2 Animals were evacuated to 15 V.E.S. The Section moved to RUE MARLE. ARMENTIERES.	

Army Form C. 2118.

WAR DIARY
or
INTELLIGENCE SUMMARY.
(Erase heading not required.)

Instructions regarding War Diaries and Intelligence Summaries are contained in F. S. Regs., Part II. and the Staff Manual respectively. Title pages will be prepared in manuscript.

Place	Date	Hour	Summary of Events and Information	Remarks and references to Appendices
ARMENTIERES.	19/10/18		D.A.D.V.S. inspected animals for Evacuation	
"	20/10/18		8 Animals were evacuated to No 15. V.E.S at STEENWEERCK. No 12992. Pte E. Cornish and No 8381. Pte J. Bovero proceeded on leave to England. The Section moved to WAMBRECHIES. Sh 36. K.2.Central	
WAMBRECHIES. 36. K.2 Central	21/10/18		All stables which had been used by the Germans were cleaned out and disinfected + all wooden mangers were removed and burnt.	
"	22/10/18		Pte J. Baker No 19761. reported back from leave. Animals for evacuation were inspected by D.A.D.V.S.	
"	23/10/18		21 Animals were evacuated to No 16 V.E.S advanced Post.	
"	24/10/18		Routine work.	
"	25/10/18		6 animals were evacuated to 15 V.E.S. advanced Post.	
"	26/10/18		No 10413. Corpl. Playford reported back from leave to England.	
"	27/10/18		Section moved to ROUBAIX. Sheet 36. F.14. c.2.4.	
"	28/10/18		No 9333 Corpl. N.J. McLaughlin and No 19761 Pte. Baker a.g. were evacuated to 135 Field Ambulance suffering from Influenza.	
ROUBAIX.	29/10/18		Routine work. D.A.D.V.S. inspected animals for Evacuation	
"	30/10/18		45 Animals were evacuated to 15. V.E.S. at LE CROIX ROUGE North East of TURCOING.	
"	31/10/18		Routine work. C.O. inspected saddlery & harness. * Rifles were Dismounted marching order parade was held when men were put thro Arms Drill Rifle drill & Rifle drill under the O.C.	

APPENDIX. P.T.O

APPENDIX. P.T.O.

WAR DIARY
or
INTELLIGENCE SUMMARY.

Army Form C. 2118.

Place	Date	Hour	Summary of Events and Information	Remarks and references to Appendices
		APPENDIX	Statement of number of Animals received during the month & how disposed of	

Nº remaining from last month. 3
Nº admitted 1/31 Oct 1918 141
           Total 144

Nº Evacuated   132
Nº Died   nil.
Nº Destroyed   1.
Nº Cured & discharged to units   4.
Stray animal found.   1
Remaining on 31/10/18   6
        TOTAL. 144

7 Evacuated
Class I Debility   55
— 9. Necrotic Dermatitis   1
— 10 Sidebones   2
    Ringbones   8
    Quittor   9
— 11. Ul. Cellulitis   9
— 12 Blind Amaurosis   12
— 13. 1st Cont.d Kick 8
   — Lacerated 6
   — Shell 11
   — Bomb 1
   Spr. Ligaments 10
   Abscess 1
   P.U.N. 4   } 44
   Undermin. Sole 3

132 Total

J. Hunt
Capt. AVC
OC 157th M.V.S.

Army Form C. 2118.

51st MOBILE VETERINARY SECTION

WAR DIARY or INTELLIGENCE SUMMARY

NOVEMBER, 1918

Place	Date	Hour	Summary of Events and Information	Remarks and references to Appendices
TOURCOING Sheet 36 F.17central	1st		All men of the Section paraded for inspection in dismounted marching order.	
	2nd		No. S.E. 9049 Sergt. Finch proceeded to England on leave.	
do	3rd		No. S.E. 9333 Cpl. McLaughlan reported for duty from 135th Field Ambulance. Seven animals were evacuated.	
"	4th		The charges of Bdr. General Hobkirk, C.M.G., D.S.O., late G.O.C. 120th Inf. Bde. was evacuated to No. 15 Veterinary Evacuation Station for despatch to Quarantine Stables, NEUFCHATEL prior to repatriation.	
"	5th		A report was received from O.C. No. 11 Casualty Clearing Station stating that No. S.E. 19761 Pte. 17 T. Baker, 17 V.C. of the Section died on 2/14/18 of Pneumonia.	
"	6th		Twenty one animals were evacuated to No. 15 V.E.S. Three nine inspected previously by the D.A.D.V.S. No. 23071 Pte. G. Daintree reported back from leave.	
"	7th		No. S.E. 14984 Pte. H. Madden proceeded on 7 days special leave to England. Routine work.	
"	8th		No. 17992 Pte. E. Annah and No. 8381 Pte. J. Bowen reported back from leave. Three animals were evacuated to No. 15 Veterinary Evacuation Station and 1 stray animal was evacuated to Field Remount Section, MENIN.	
"	9th		A dismounted marching order parade of the Section and rifle inspection took place, also a harness and vehicle inspection.	

510Y M.V.S.

WAR DIARY or **INTELLIGENCE SUMMARY**

Army Form C. 2118.

Nov. 1918.

Place	Date	Hour	Summary of Events and Information	Remarks and references to Appendices
TOURCOING	10th		Six animals were evacuated.	
"	11th		No. T.T. 03720 Pte. A. Abbott reported for duty from No. 2 Veterinary Hospital.	
"	12th		No. 1310 Pte. J. Haydock who was despatched to No. 2 Vety. Hospital to perform Routine work.	
"	13th		No. 25934 Pte. H. Clavely reported for duty from No. 2 Vety. Hospital.	
"	14th		No. 25707 Pte. J. Barrett proceeded on leave to England.	
"	15th		No. 30426 Pte. G. Bromhead was admitted to 135th Field Ambulance with Venereal Malaise.	
"	16/17/18		Seven animals were evacuated. Routine work.	
"	19th		One mare (of 136 Field Ambulance) died. Post mortem was made cause of death was (stoppage) Gentents.	
"	20th		Ten animals were evacuated.	
CROIX	21st		The Section moved to CROIX (Sheet 36/L 4 d 4.4).	
"	22nd		The A.D.V.S. XIVth Corps and the D.A.D.V.S. inspected the Section.	
"	23rd		Two animals were evacuated.	
"	24th		Sergt. Lynch reported back from leave. No. 8381 Pte. J. Borrero was admitted to 135th Field Ambulance suffering from Contusion. Head, the result of an accident.	
"	25th		Two animals were evacuated.	
"	26th		Routine work	

51st M.V.S.

Army Form C. 2118.

WAR DIARY
or
INTELLIGENCE SUMMARY.

Nov. 1918

Place	Date	Hour	Summary of Events and Information	Remarks and references to Appendices
CROIX	27th		Pte. Bonner was discharged from 137th Field Ambulance.	
"	28th		Three animals were evacuated.	
"	29th		Routine work.	
"	30th		1 mange case was evacuated to No. 15 Veterinary Section. The Scheme for Demobilization and the facilities for educational training pending demobilization were explained to the men and names were taken of those desirous of attending the classes.	

51 M.V.S.

WAR DIARY
or
INTELLIGENCE SUMMARY.
(Erase heading not required.)

Nov. 1918

Army Form C. 2118.

IV

APPENDIX.

Statement of number of animals received and how disposed of.

Remaining from last month = 6
Admitted — 94
Total — 100

Evacuated — 86
Died — 1
Strays issued — 3
Remaining on 30/11/18 — 10
Total — 100

Class I: Debility — 24

Class VI: Colic — 1

Class IX { Mange — 4
{ Necrotic Derm — 1

Class X { Lotilo — 2
{ Ringbone — 1
{ Sidebone — 2
{ Laminitis — 1
{ Arthritis — 6

Class XI: Mal. Cellulitis — 8
Class XII: Anaemia — 4
Class VIII (Wound cont. — 1
   " Amety — 1
   " Lacerated — 5
   " front — 8 Portugal
   " Punctured — 6
   " Kicks — 2
   " Strain Ligts — 12
   " P.U.N.
   " Sore Back — 86
   For Repatriation

J. Hughes Capt. A.V.C.
O.C. 51st M.V.S.

1/12/18

No. 5/ or Mobile Veterinary Section

WAR DIARY
or
INTELLIGENCE SUMMARY.
(Erase heading not required.)

Army Form C. 2118

December 1918

Place	Date	Hour	Summary of Events and Information	Remarks and references to Appendices
CRUIT Sheet 36 L.4C/47	1st		Seven animals were evacuated to No. 15 Veterinary Evacuation Station.	
"	2nd		Pte. Barnett reported back from leave.	
"	3rd		Routine Work	
"	4th		Four animals were evacuated to No. 15 V.E.S.	
"	5th 6th 7th		Routine Work. Animals for evacuation were inspected by the D.A.D.V.S. Fourteen animals were evacuated to No. 15 V.E.S.	
"	8th		No. 28263 Pte. A. Moore reported from No. 2 Veterinary Hospital and was taken on the strength.	
"	9th		Eight animals were evacuated to No. 15 V.E.S.	
"	10th		Routine work	
"	11th 12th			
"	13th		A Board of Survey, President Major Petro, OC No. 1 Coy, H.S.C., assembled to check the equipment of the Section. Two troop mares of the Section were sent to WAMBRECHIES for re-training.	

51 MVS

Army Form C. 2118.

WAR DIARY
or
INTELLIGENCE SUMMARY.
(Erase heading not required.)

Place	Date	Hour	Summary of Events and Information	Remarks and references to Appendices
CROIX	14th 15th		Routine Work.	
"	16th		Animals for evacuation were inspected by the D.A.D.V.S.	
"	17th		Twenty two animals were evacuated to No. 15 V.E.S.	
"	19th		Thirteen animals were evacuated.	
"	20th		One horse (B/932 Labour Coy.) was returned to its unit cured.	
"	22nd		Fifteen animals were evacuated.	
"	23rd/th		Routine Work.	
"	27th		Twenty three animals were evacuated to No. 15 V.E.S.	
"	29th		Twenty four animals were evacuated.	
"	30th		Routine work.	
"	31st		No. S.E. 8351 Pte. J. Borrows proceeded to BRUSSELS on four days leave.	

51/MVS

Army Form C. 2118.

WAR DIARY
or
INTELLIGENCE SUMMARY.
(Erase heading not required.)

Instructions regarding War Diaries and Intelligence Summaries are contained in F.S. Regs., Part II. and the Staff Manual respectively. Title pages will be prepared in manuscript.

Place	Date	Hour	Summary of Events and Information	Remarks and references to Appendices
			Statement showing number of animals received during the month pins disposed of	

Remaining on 31/11/18
Unfit for service 10
.... 189
Total 199

Discharged
Evacuated 193
To Mule breed 2
Pied 1
.... 3
Remaining 1/1/19 .... —
Total 199

Class I Debility 83

Class II
Rheum 2
Catarrh 2 4

Class IX
Mange 29
Grease 4
Ringworm 1 34

Class X
Exhaustion 1
Saddle sore 2
Sprain 7
Girth 3 13

Class XI Tubercular 4

Class XII
Eyes 31
Ophthalmia 1 32

Class XIII
Wound lacerated 1
Contused 12
Punctured 1
P.V.N. 1
Abscess 3
Sp muscle 2
Sp Tendons 2 22

Total 193

Munro
Capt. A.V.C.
O.C. 51 M.V.S.

Army Form C. 2118.

WAR DIARY
or
INTELLIGENCE SUMMARY.
(Erase heading not required.)

51 Mob Vety Sec

Vol 3 3

Place	Date	Hour	Summary of Events and Information	Remarks and references to Appendices
Camp Steur-36	1st		Thirty two animals were evacuated to No. 15 Veterinary Evacuation Station.	
L d'A?	2nd		No. 2228 I Pte. T. Owens proceeded on leave to England. Brood mares of the eleven were received for evacuation	
	3rd		Fourteen Brood mares evacuated to No. 15 Veterinary Evacuation Station. Three of them in charge of and two mules and animals belonging to this section. Three sick animals were also evacuated.	
	4th		Thirteen brood mares evacuated to No. 15 Veterinary Evacuation Station	
	5th		Forty four animals evacuated to No. 15 Veterinary Evacuation Station	
	6th 7th		Routine Work	
	8th		Pte Bowen reported back from leave to England (10-1-19 to 24-1-19). No. 11952 Sergt Brown proceeded on leave to England	
	9th		Eighteen animals were evacuated to No 15 Veterinary Evacuation Station Routine Work	
	10th		Fifteen animals were evacuated to No. 15 Veterinary Evacuation Station	

Army Form C. 2118.

WAR DIARY
or
INTELLIGENCE SUMMARY.
(Erase heading not required.)

Instructions regarding War Diaries and Intelligence Summaries are contained in F. S. Regs., Part II. and the Staff Manual respectively. Title pages will be prepared in manuscript.

Place	Date	Hour	Summary of Events and Information	Remarks and references to Appendices
	11th		No. 0567 Corporal Bonny reported from No 2 Veterinary Hospital for duty (AVC Records 22/3240/18 dated 24/2/18.	
	12th		Routine Work	
	13		Pte A. Abbott admitted to 137 Field Ambulance suffering from Otorhoea. N o 1073 Corps	
			Playfoot proceeded to No 2 Veterinary Hospital Havre	
	14th		Routine work	
	15th		Seventeen animals were evacuated to No 15 Veterinary Evacuation Station	
	16		No. 22808 Pte Veale proceeded on leave to England (18-1-19 to 1-2-19)	
			One horse of the French Army was evacuated to No 15 Veterinary Evacuation Station	
	17		Pte Abbott was discharged from 137 Field Ambulance	
	18		S.A.D.V.S. inspected the section and fifteen animals which were evacuated to No 15 Veterinary Evacuation Station	
	19		Routine Work	
	20		No 8381 Pte J Bowers sentenced to seven days No 2 Field Punishment for being absent from 21.30 to 22.30 on the 17-1-19. Being in Rouveaux without a pass.	
	21st		Animals for Evacuation. Fourteen animals evacuated to No 15 Veterinary Evacuation Station. D.A.D.V.S. inspected Viva Animals	

WAR DIARY
or
INTELLIGENCE SUMMARY

Army Form C. 2118.

Place	Date	Hour	Summary of Events and Information	Remarks and references to Appendices
	22nd		Pte Owen reported sick while on leave (London doctor's certificate enclosed)	
	23rd		Six animals from the French Army evacuated to No 15 Veterinary Evacuation Stn. T/06/9012 Dr Spearman R.A.S.C. proceeded on leave to England (25-1-19 to 8-2-19). No 259734 Pte 6 Lowry was admitted to 135 F. Ambulance suffering from influenza. Mules drawn transferred to No 15 Veterinary Evacuation Station. One	
	24th		horse of the French Army. Pte Bamford returned to 'H' Group C.C. for hearing out of camp when a horse.	
	25th		Animals of the Section were classified by the Veterinary Board. Four animals were sold to publishers at regulation price of £1.25 to public.	
	26th		Eight horses and one mule were evacuated to No 15 Veterinary Evacuation Station. Three returned to French Army.	
	27th		Four horses were destroyed for hiding purposes.	
	28th		Six horses were destroyed for hiding. Pte Nunn proceeded on leave to England (30-1-19 to 13-2-19)	
	29th		Remount Board classification. The animals of the Section	
	30th		Two Surrendered animals were evacuated to No 15 Veterinary Evacuation Station	

Army Form C. 2118.

WAR DIARY
or
INTELLIGENCE SUMMARY.
(Erase heading not required.)

Instructions regarding War Diaries and Intelligence Summaries are contained in F. S. Regs., Part II. and the Staff Manual respectively. Title pages will be prepared in manuscript.

Place	Date	Hour	Summary of Events and Information	Remarks and references to Appendices
	30		Sergt. Brown admitted to 30th General Hospital while returning from leave suffering from influenza.	
	31		Drivers discharged 4 and 2 of this section were influenza. Ptc (A/Capt.) McLaughlin RAMC and Dr. Stewart RASC left this unit for the institution base on demobilization.	

S. Hunt
Capt. R.A.V.C.
O.C. 512st Mobile Vety
Section.

1/2/19.

A.5831. Wt W4973/M687 750,000 8/16 D.D.&L. Ltd. Forms/C.2118/13.

WAR DIARY or INTELLIGENCE SUMMARY

Army Form C. 2118.

51 Mob Vety Sec

WD Sep 3 4

Place	Date	Hour	Summary of Events and Information	Remarks and references to Appendices
CROIX Sheet 36 L.40/4.1	1st		Routine work	
	2nd		No. 5940 S.S. Bowyer R.A.V.C. Regt. Shaw on demobilisation. 10 A.V.N.S. visited Section	
	3rd		Three animals sold for butchery. Four horses of French Army evacuated to 15 V.E.S.	
	4th		No. 9865 Serj. Smith R.A.V.C. reported for duty from No. 2 Vet. Hosp. Two animals sold for butchery	
	5th		10 A.V.N.S. visited Section and inspected animals for evacuation. Nineteen animals were evacuated to 15 V.E.S. including one French horse. Thirty one horses from 265th Regt. 10th Artillerie de Campagne, French Army, were admitted to this Section	
	6th		10 A.V.N.S. visited Section and inspected French animals & others. Twenty six horses were admitted from 135th Regt. Artillerie Lourde, French Army. Fifty six animals were evacuated to 15 V.E.S. including fifty two French animals. Five of the French animals admitted on the 5th inst. were discharged	
	7th		Five animals sold for butchery. Three animals were evacuated to 15 V.E.S. including two French animals which were admitted this day from 135 Regt. Artillerie Lourde. 10th McDowell R.A.V.C. was admitted to 131 Field Amb. France	
	8th		Five animals were admitted, including two French animals, from 13th Key 1st Regt. R.E. 97. and one from 265th R.A.C. A.1st Battery. The two from 15th C.G.P. Art. R.E. were evacuated	
	9th		10 A.V.N.S. visited the Section & inspected animals for evacuation	
	10th		10/4 Medic. R.A.V.C. reported back from leave to U.K. One horse was sold for butchery. Six animals were evacuated, including one French horse	
	11th		Nine horses admitted, including four French horses. 10 A.V.N.S. visited Section and inspected animals for evacuation	

Army Form C. 2118.

WAR DIARY
or
INTELLIGENCE SUMMARY.
(Erase heading not required.)

Instructions regarding War Diaries and Intelligence Summaries are contained in F. S. Regs., Part II. and the Staff Manual respectively. Title pages will be prepared in manuscript.

Place	Date	Hour	Summary of Events and Information	Remarks and references to Appendices
CROIX Sheet 36 L40/47	Feb. 12th		Nine horses evacuated to 15th V.E.S. including four French horses. 10/e Madden proceeded to Lille, to compete in VI Army Jumping Competition, and was accompanied by 10/e Rowntree. Two French horses were admitted.	
	13th		10/e Barnett & No 25707 was admitted to No M.R.&S. from 134 Field Ambulance. Sergt Smith, 10/ses Rainham, Neale, Rossi, Rowntree & Cuthew R.A.V.C. and 10/e Ashdown R.A.S.B. (attached) were admitted to 134 Field Ambulance.	
	14th		Capt Hunter R.A.V.C. and 10/e Madden were admitted to 101 Field Ambulance. Capt Slough R.A.V.C. took over the charge of the Section. Seven animals were admitted, including four French animals. Eleven animals were evacuated to 15th V.E.S. including six French horses. These were evacuated by 10 C.D.N.S.	
	15th		Four animals were evacuated to 15th V.E.S.	
	16th		Routine work.	
	17th		Seven animals admitted. Three animals evacuated to 15th V.E.S. 10 C.D.N.S. visited Section.	
	18th		Four animals admitted. Seven animals evacuated to 15th V.E.S.	
	19th		Two animals admitted.	
	20th		Four animals admitted including one French horse. Two animals sold for Butchery. Two animals admitted. Six animals evacuated to 15th V.E.S. One animal sold for Butchery.	
	21st		One French horse admitted on 20th developed acute Laminitis and was too lame to travel and was destroyed.	

WAR DIARY or INTELLIGENCE SUMMARY

Army Form C. 2118

Place	Date	Hour	Summary of Events and Information	Remarks and references to Appendices
CROIX Sheet 36 L40/47	22nd		Seven animals were admitted and evacuated to 15th VES. Notification received from No XI CCS. T4 do878 10m O/S down RASC attached to 51st MVS. died on 20-2-1919 of Influenza, a Broncho-Pneumonia.	
	23rd		10/e Moore C. No 28260 reported from leave to UK. Remaining men granted seven days extension by A.B.4.(F) War Office (A.F.W.3260). 10 A.10 N.S. visited Section. No SE 3016 Sergt Willshar RAVC reported for duty from No 4 Vet. Hosp. Calais.	
	24th		Twenty horses of 12th Regt Chasseurs, French Army were admitted, & evacuated same day to 15th VES.	
	25th		Two horses of 2nd Regt Chasseurs French Army were admitted. No 10389 SS Betelhume RAVC reported for duty from No 2 Vet Hosp. Boulogne. No 22801. 10/e Owens RAVC, and No 3012 10/e Yorman RAVC reported back from leave to UK. 10 A.10 N.S. visited Section. Sergt Shuntli RAVC No 8155 Sergt Small, L 1952, Sergt Brown 10/es Hurst Mardlin 43071 Loundes, 63720 Whelen, 25718 Shirtliam, 22108 Rossio, 25934 Wealthy 25707 Yeoman, 72108 Neale, Rawing, keen were evacuated sick, as Struck off the Strength and horse Records notified.	
	26th		Seven animals were evacuated to 15th VES. This includes one French Horse.	
	27th		One French Horse was evacuated to 15th VES. This was not accepted and notification was sent, about by order of DDVS. 5th Army arrangements were to be made for the liberty animals of the 12th Regt Chasseurs, evacuated on the 24th Inst. to be returned to this Section.	
	28th		Three animals Sold for Butchery. Twenty horses received from 3rd Regt Chasseurs on 25-2-19 returned to their owner. Twenty horses received from 12th Regt Chasseurs, French Army on the 24th Inst. A evacuated to 15th VES same day, were returned to this Section. 10 A.10 N.S. visited the Section.	

R tu Hugh
Capt RAVC
O/C 51st MVS

Army Form C. 2118.

WAR DIARY
or
INTELLIGENCE SUMMARY.
(Erase heading not required.)

Instructions regarding War Diaries and Intelligence Summaries are contained in F.S. Regs., Part II. and the Staff Manual respectively. Title pages will be prepared in manuscript.

Place	Date MARCH	Hour	Summary of Events and Information	Remarks and references to Appendices
51st Mobile Veterinary Section. Vroix.	1		4 identity horses, admitted on 24th Feb. from 12th Regt. de Chasseurs, (French Army) were returned to their Unit. No. 9049 Sergt. French left this Unit, for No. 2 Vet. Hosp. Havre, for tour of stone duty.	
	2			
	3		No. 28263 X0/c Moore A. left this Unit on demobilisation	
			Six animals evacuated to No. 15 V.E.S. One animal sold for Butchery.	
	4		One LD. horse, category Z. evacuated to LINSELLES Collecting Camp. Telegram from No. 20 Genl. Hospital Capt. Hamilton R.A.V.C. evacuated to Boufond 4.3.19. 10 Q. 10 V.S. visited the Section.	
	5		One animal sold for Butchery. Four animals evacuated to No. 15 V.E.S. One animal admitted.	
	6		One animal admitted.	
	7		Two animals evacuated to 15th V.E.S. Three animals admitted. 10 Q. 10 V.S. visited the Section.	
	8		Two Section horses R1 category "Y" evacuated to TOURCOING Camp.	
	9		One animal admitted. 10 Q. 10 V.S. visited the Section.	
	10		Two horses sold for Butchery. Four animals evacuated to 15th V.E.S. Three animals admitted	
	11		10 Q. 10 V.S. visited the Section. Four animals admitted	
	12		Seven animals evacuated to No. 15 V.E.S. One horse admitted.	
	13		Two animals admitted. Sergt. Wiltshire S.S. Butchers R.A.V.C. and Pte Branagen R.F.A. were admitted for being in an Estaminet during prohibited hours. (ARO 2300). 10 Q. 10 V.S. visited the Section.	
	14		Routine work.	
	15		Three animals were admitted. Five animals evacuated to 15th V.E.S	
	16		One animal admitted.	
	17		One horse admitted. One mule sold for Butchery.	

Army Form C. 2118.

WAR DIARY
or
INTELLIGENCE SUMMARY.
(Erase heading not required.)

Instructions regarding War Diaries and Intelligence Summaries are contained in F. S. Regs., Part II. and the Staff Manual respectively. Title pages will be prepared in manuscript.

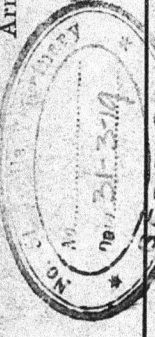

Place	Date	Hour	Summary of Events and Information	Remarks and references to Appendices
51st Mobile Veterinary Section	MARCH 18		Three animals admitted, one horse sold for butchery	
	19		Three animals evacuated to 15th V.E.S. One animal admitted	
	20		7702188 Sergt Stavis R.A.V.C. attached to 39th M.G.B. having become surplus, reported for duty to this Section. One horse admitted	
	21		Two Section Horses L.D category X. evacuated to LINSELLES Camp	
	22		9/4 09 3012. Dvr Norman R.A.S.C. attached to this unit, RASC AUTH 8cdys 40th 10w Train, was returned to N° 2 Coy 40th 10w sub Train. Four animals evacuated to 15 V.E.S. This includes on Section Horse R2 category AX which was evacuated sick. One horse sold for butchery	
	23		Two Section Horses R2 category X. evacuated to TOURCOING Camp, also one X Horse from 39th M.G.B.	
	24		Two horses evacuated to 15th V.E.S	
	25. & 26.		Routine work.	
	27.		7702188. Sergt Stavis R.A.V.C left this Section for concent. 1. St. Andre, on demobilisation	
	28/29/30		Routine work.	
	31.		The following Sergts R.A.V.C. having become surplus to these units have been posted to this unit and taken on the Strength from this date. SE 8803 Sergt W. Roe 2 V.E. attached 64th B.A.C., 11882 Sergt Bedby E.A. attached 64th A.F.A. Regt. SE 25579 Sergt Clark A.A. attached A/64th Army Bgd. R.F.A.	

P. M. Haigh
Capt. RAVC
O.C. 51st MVS

www.ingramcontent.com/pod-product-compliance
Lightning Source LLC
Chambersburg PA
CBHW081544160426
43191CB00011B/1832